The TEEN TOOLBOX

Equipping Parents and Teenagers with the Tools for **Navigating Adolescence**

CAI GRAHAM

RETHINK PRESS

First published in Great Britain 2017
by Rethink Press (www.rethinkpress.com)

© Copyright Cai Graham

Praise for *"The Teen Toolbox"*

"If you're wondering how to get your teen to talk to you, how to connect with them again and feel like you don't know where you went wrong then you are in safe hands with the book you are holding in yours. I highly recommend you grab this chance to discover an approach to your teenagers that will bring more harmony to your home and strength, love and fun back to your family. Cai Graham has masterfully created a guide for mums and dads to enjoy the years of parenting a teen – rather than endure them. Read this book – your kids, one day, will thank you."

Katharine Dever, mum of three,
entrepreneur and writer

"What I can see is it's clear and it's clear it's needed! It's horrific how many kids are prescribed medication when the solution is simple (not easy) so thank goodness for this clear and informative book – it's like Cai is holding your hand and guiding you on how to help your kids and yourself, have a better relationship and a happier life."

Marion Bevington, award-winning public
speaking mentor, founder of Stage Fright Away

"As a parent of teenagers myself, I fully understand many of the challenges that families have to encounter throughout the adolescent years; though simple, many of the solutions that Cai recommends are easy and fast to adopt. This is a valuable point of reference for all parents wanting to reconnect with their teenager and embrace this stage of parenthood with more confidence."

Andy Harrington, Sunday Times
best-selling author of Passion Into Profit,
www.passionintoprofit.co.uk

"Cai Graham's book is a brilliant go-to manual when you feel you have no answers to your children's behaviour. Her sensible approach to parenting – with easily remembered phrases and advice – is just what we all need when we get stressed as parents. I was particularly moved by the advice to be mindful how we phrase certain things to young adults. Words really resonate with teenagers and we need to change our behaviour as well as encouraging them to behave better. And most importantly, I love that Cai says it's ok to take time out to look after ourselves. I'd recommend this book to every parent I know."

Denise Watson, radio presenter
and sports journalist

"While my own children were obviously perfect in every way... boy could I have done with Cai Graham's *Teen Toolbox* – the teen blue print, role models, setting boundaries, the perils of peer pressure… and then there's sex, drugs, drink and social media. Its easily navigated, and provides an empowering affirmation that we have it within ourselves to cope."

Wendy Austin, Inside Business,
BBC Radio Ulster

"With my daughter about to turn 12, *The Teen Toolbox* is my essential preparatory playbook to help me navigate the coming chaos. Cai Graham has nailed it with this book, giving us parents a clear blueprint to understanding the heart and mind of our teenager so that rather than seeming to thwart their happiness, we can help them thrive! Essential, eye-opening reading!"

James Lavers, digital educator,
founder of Lazy Coach

"Once I started *The Teen Toolbox,* I couldn't put it down. As the father of two young boys, I found the book to be incredibly useful for me as a parent. The book covers the major spectrum of family dynamics and expertly addresses the core issues faced by teenagers and their respective parents. The book didn't just highlight these issues, it also provided practical easy to use solutions to resolve them as well. This book in my personal opinion is a 'MUST' read for Parents of all ages and also for teachers and teenagers themselves."

Tosin Ogunnusi, UK's number 1
empowerment activities trainer

CONTENTS

Chapter 16
Minimising Conflict

Chapter 17
Sex, Drugs and Drink

Introduction

Why this book?

You

OK, so you've picked up this book, and you've probably done so because you've got some concerns about parenting a teenager. But don't see it as an admission of defeat or a sign that a family relationship is on the skids. It just means you care, and because of that you want to make some positive changes.

I know this because it's reflected in what the parents who come to me say time and again. Sometimes the concern is framed in a positive way:

- ✿ I'm looking for a closer relationship with my teen.
- ✿ I'd like the happy family life that other people seem to have.
- ✿ I want to create a safer environment for my child.

And sometimes it's focused on the difficulties of family life:

- ✿ Why is my child getting angrier and angrier?
- ✿ Why does our house feel as if it's filled with a constant barrage of slanging matches?
- ✿ We don't seem to have happy family mealtimes, let alone family holidays.
- ✿ I seem to be backing down all the time just to keep the peace.

Rather than get carried away with all the possible negatives, I want to distil the main messages that emerge from the diverse family dynamics and experiences I see every day.

Parents, by and large, just want their teenagers to be happy. Once the hormones kick in and teenagers start the often painful journey towards independence from their families, it can seem as if they are mounting a campaign of wilful opposition. Parents may worry that saying no to their teenagers will jeopardise the relationship, and may yearn for the calmer, happier family lives they had with younger, less challenging children.

The teenagers themselves may feel thwarted at every turn. They may want to be simultaneously understood and left alone to get on with it — a tall order from the parents' point of view. No matter how stable their family background, teenagers will be riddled with insecurities. It comes with the territory of being an adolescent. Increasingly, they may be aware that there is a whole new world out there — a world of proliferating drugs, media channels, technology — that their parents simply can't keep pace with. This leaves both parties feeling vulnerable. Teenagers are often given bad press, and I want to redress that balance a bit because it's not their fault. Invariably, it's down to hormones and biology and compounded by parents who are ill-equipped to deal with them or who may even be struggling with their own baggage.

At the moment, you may feel as if your relationship with your child is an absolute train wreck. Much as other approaches — such as cognitive behavioural therapy or counselling – focus on the whole person rather than a specific problem, I think that would be a mistake in this context. Your relationship with your child is probably nowhere near as bad as you think. You wouldn't consign a car to the scrap heap for having a flat tyre; you'd just get it fixed. Similarly, you just need to fix up the specific problems that have arisen between you and your child. And it's not so much repairing damage as re-establishing a link.

I'm aiming to provide practical solutions to problems that are common to a lot of families.

The majority of parents who first approach me say, 'Can you help my child? They're just not listening to me.' Or, 'Will you sort my child out? I'm lost as to how to do it myself.'

Thing is — it's invariably not the child who is 'broken'. Nine times out of ten there is an overall breakdown in the family unit. So truth be told, the buck stops with the parents and not the children.

I help parents to communicate again: with themselves, with their partners, and ultimately with their children. This makes for a much stronger and healthier family, and in the longer term, these changes tend to span more than one generation. How cool is that?

So how would you like to feel after reading this book?

I want you to

- ❖ feel safe in the knowledge that your child loves you,
- ❖ be able to make informed decisions, and
- ❖ be confident that your decisions are the right ones, for all in your family.

What this book will provide you with is a practical set of techniques to enable you to take control, cut through the chaos, and regain your closeness to your child.

Regardless of age, we all have three basic needs: to be **loved**, to be **understood**, and to be **respected**. Once a child starts feeling that a parent is fulfilling these needs, the changes — and the rewards — are huge. Many of the exercises in this book address these basic needs.

Me

What are my credentials? Well, I'm a mum — a mum of two kids whose adolescent years are not that far behind them. I'm a master practitioner of neuro-linguistic programming (NLP), so I come armed with the theoretical knowledge behind improved communications. I've been a ChildLine counsellor, so I have experience addressing the wide range of problems and anxieties children face. I've also been a volunteer for Home-Start, the UK's leading family support charity.

But I've also been a child, of course. I had a great childhood — an unhappy early childhood is not a prerequisite for teenage insecurity and anxiety. It's just that I felt I had no voice. Admittedly, in my generation there was still a bit of a view that children should be seen and not heard, which is not a constructive approach. The reason why I focus on the adolescent age group is that I remember what it feels like to be at that stage of life.

The insecurities of my adolescence are still gut-wrenchingly vivid. I can trace the source of my low self-confidence to an incident that took place when I was ten. At a parent-teacher evening at my school, I was sitting with my mum and dad in front of my favourite teacher — she looked like Julie Andrews. She peered at my parents patronisingly, sort of shook her head, and said, 'Well, Caroline isn't really going to be setting the Thames on fire, is she?'

My whole world came crashing down. I had thought I was good, that I was all right, and suddenly, in my mind, here was my teacher saying, 'She's thick, she's stupid, she's below average.' In fact, there was nothing wrong with me at all, but when she said that, I felt that I was mediocre — substandard, in fact.

It was only after I started doing NLP that I realised I'd been carrying that statement around with me for thirty-five years. As adults, we have to remember that a throwaway line can absolutely cripple a child if we're not careful. It was a throwaway comment, I think, but to me, as a child, the words were cruel. I believed her. I thought she was the expert.

Shortage of resources

I would say that 30% of 'children' I see aged between ten to twenty-five don't come back to me after their initial free consultation. This is because during our chat, I explain a) a bit about biological changes they are experiencing, and b) what life as an adolescent involves, and they then realise that they're coping all right.

Sometimes the problem is more that parents are overreacting, than that teenagers are getting out of hand. Half the battle is maintaining perspective and understanding that adolescence can be a journey across uncharted waters, and that your challenge is to navigate through a few of the choppier stretches. Your experience at the moment doesn't mean that your relationship with your child is doomed.

I recently had a conversation with a group of twenty-one-year-olds sitting round a table. It transpired that about 60% of them were currently on, or had recently been prescribed, anti-depressants. I asked a couple of GPs some days later, 'What on earth's going on? Why are so many young people being put on pills and anti-depressants?' They replied, 'Because GPs don't actually have the resources to sit down and talk to these kids about what's bothering them.' If we had the luxury of enough GPs with hour-long slots for each patient, and shorter waiting lists for CAMHS (Child and Adolescent Mental Health Services) the majority of these kids would not have to be on anti-depressants in the first place. (There is a report in my app that you can read on this topic. It provides practical steps to help.)

An epidemic?

 Between 2005 and 2012, there was a 54% increase in the number of young people prescribed anti-depressants in the UK.

European Journal of
Neuropsychopharmacology

I don't want to get political, but schools are oversubscribed, counsellors are stretched to the limit, and CAMHS is buckling under the strain. This is why I want to move away from offering one-to-one support, through which I can reach only a few people, and move to an approach that will allow me to help many more young people. Of course, there will always be extreme cases which must be dealt with through professional medical intervention, but often, all that young people really need is a conversation with someone. My experience at ChildLine proves that. Callers often sign off with, 'I'm fine now. Thanks for listening.' They, too, realise they're not doing so badly after all.

Parents

I hear a lot of parents say things along the lines of, 'My child was absolutely fine at primary school, and now they're at secondary school, the wheels have come off,' or 'They don't seem to want to talk to me anymore', or 'What have I done wrong?' … Does any of this sound familiar? Well, that's actually meant to happen. It's all about the child's need for independence. It's about the child's separation from the family.

It does not mean that the relationship between parent and child is irreparably broken; but there are things that can be done to ensure that the lines of communication can remain open, which in turn will help to alleviate some of the concerns – on both sides.

I understand where these children are coming from. How embarrassing to tell your mum and dad what's going on — especially when it might turn out to be nothing much after all! However, the child themselves can misinterpret the situation. They think that their parents are too busy, or that they won't understand — after all, they clearly came out of the Ark. Remember also, that just perhaps, it's that the parents themselves are the problem.

But, all too often, parents are likely to take the child's reluctance to confide in them personally. It is therefore helpful to take your egos out of this equation and simply say, 'Listen, I'm still here for you. I know you don't want to talk to me, but when you do, or if you do, I'm here.'

The sooner you start to communicate with and understand your child, the better. It's easier to help a child through a couple of hurdles in life than mend a broken adult. Helping adults with issues of self-worth, self-belief, and self-confidence, to name but a few, is hard work, whereas kids, if caught at the right time, are able to embrace the notion 'It's all right to be myself'. You might even quote Dr Seuss: 'Why fit in when you were born to stand out?'

When I said these words to one girl, she got it instantly, answering, 'Oh my God, yeah, that's right! It doesn't matter that I am different from everyone else!' She was a new child after that. So, catching children young is important if you want them to like who they see in the mirror. Too many adults don't, and it's harder to break down those barriers once someone's got years of self-hatred under his or her belt.

As my darling dad used to say, 'Life is not a dress rehearsal.' You only get one chance. You could wait, but what's the point? You may as well just grasp the nettle and get on with it because the longer you leave something to stew, the harder it is to fix.

How to use this book

The principles, and the exercises based on them, featured in this book have worked for me. Many of them I discovered later on, and I rather wish I'd had them at my fingertips when my own children were still teenagers. A lot of what I'm saying is obvious, but sometimes, when you feel you can't see the wood for the trees, you need someone else to hit the brakes for you and say, 'Listen, just stop and think. Do this.' The point is, it might be stating the obvious, but are you doing it?

The first half of the book sets out the principles, and the second half of the book focuses on specific problems and features a number of practical exercises and techniques. If you read a little bit and then do a little bit, you'll gain a greater understanding than you would if you just read this book from cover to cover. It's a workbook, really, so pick it up, put it down, write in the margins, underline the bits that you want to come back to, etc. By reviewing sections and revisiting exercises, you'll form the habits — you'll hardwire the bits that work best for you. You'll also get insight into how you can quickly build a stronger relationship with your child. Many of these exercises are based on NLP techniques. They are quick and easy to implement. You'll come to recognise which exercises resonate well with you; and with repetition some of the techniques will soon become second nature. These exercises are fast, easy to remember and above all, child friendly – so you should also consider sharing them with your child. They will thank you for it.

To help you navigate this book, I've included this symbol that denotes an exercise or technique for you and your child to practice.

I have another free resource, which is my App; also called The TEEN Toolbox. It has many of these exercises included, and much more besides.

To download the app - please visit your app store and search for TEEN Toolbox.

PART I

Chapter 1

The Golden Rules

Life is 10% what happens to you and 90% how you react to it.

———————————— Charles R. Swindoll ————

Though we may doubt ourselves, we all have the inner resources to take on the problems that arise in our families. Much of it is common sense, but it's amazing how hard it can be to access common sense when you feel you are losing control. This is why I'm here as your tour guide. I'll set out the theoretical foundation for what you need to do, and give you the tools and techniques for doing it. In return, you may have to dig deep and do the hard work. When you feel overwhelmed, say to yourself, 'I can do this, and I will do this.'

The principles below set out the rationale for my approach and illustrate how it works. I'm sure you will recognise that some of these principles are already operating in your life.

Old ways of thinking have to go

It doesn't matter who said it — the meaning is the same:

> 66 If you always do what you've always done, you will always get what you've always got.

Your current way of thinking has got you to where you are now, so the only way forward, the only way to get more positive results, is to change your way of thinking. Reshaping habitual thought patterns is crucial, and we will explore mindset in greater detail in the next chapter. Believe me, we all have the capability to make this change.

With change come opportunities

Kids fear the uncertainty change brings (come to think of it, so do many adults). It could be going to a new school or going to university, changing friend groups, or trying out a new club or class. We have to encourage kids to embrace and accept change. Yes, it can be challenging, but the opportunities are the greater for it. By encouraging them to cope with that change and acknowledging that there are opportunities, you'll help their confidence grow so that they can navigate all that uncertainty and enjoy the feeling of coming out on the other side.

What you focus on, you attract

Focus on 'I want a family that gets on better,' or 'I want to have stronger relationships with my kids,' rather than 'I don't want to be fighting all the time.' This is because the unconscious mind does not work with negatives. If I say 'Don't think of a pink elephant' you instantly think of a pink elephant. We must guide the mind into thinking in positive ways rather than negative ones. Keep your attention on what you're looking for and on the brighter future ahead; don't let the negativity you're seeking to move away from hold you back. You could sum it up as 'eyes on the prize'.

Suspend your critical mind

To maintain the positive focus, you need to suspend your critical mind. Think of watching a Superman film. You say to yourself, almost without realising it, 'I know a man can't fly, and I know there's no such thing as kryptonite, but I'm just going to go with the flow here.' I'm asking you to trust the process because this book contains techniques that have proven successful for many people. Give them a whirl and see what happens.

We cannot change another person

It's important to remember that we cannot change another person; we can only change ourselves. A useful formula sums up the process behind this fact:

EVENT + RESPONSE = OUTCOME

As this equation demonstrates, if we want a different outcome, the only thing that we can do is change our own response to the event. Rather than trying to change our teenager's behaviour, we must work on our response to it. In fact, I'd go so far as to say — and it's a bold statement — that any breakdown in the relationship with the child is the adult's problem, not the child's. So it's up to you, the parent, to acknowledge this: 'Right, I am the adult here, so I am the one who needs to make changes.' The teenager has probably got so much other crap going on that if no one takes control of the situation, it's just going to be the same old, same old.

Positive intention

In fraught family situations, we need to look behind our own behaviour and the child's and work out what the positive intention is. Even though the adult might think that the child is being difficult, whether they know it or not, the child is fulfilling an imperative; they must assert an identity that is separate from the family. In turn, what the teenager needs to understand is that the unconscious mind is set on keeping us safe, on looking after us daily. So the parental mind is saying, 'Right, well, I kept you [the child] safe yesterday, and you're still alive, so let's do today exactly the same as we did yesterday.' That is the parent's positive intention, frustrating though it can be to the teenager.

Other people see the world differently

As adults, we have a wealth of experience behind us, so we see things very differently from our children. We can see the bigger picture; they often can't. This is not to say that one perspective is right and the other wrong. It's just saying that you can't judge until you have 'walked a mile' in someone else's shoes. Other perspectives have to be acknowledged and respected. And precisely because we are the adults, and we have the broader perspective, we are also responsible for taking the initiative in making positive changes.

The magic of thinking small

Just in case all this seems a bit overwhelming, I want to remind you of an old joke. How do you eat an elephant (the pink one, perhaps)? One bite at a time. By taking baby steps you can achieve huge changes. The tiny changes that Sir Dave Brailsford made to the Team GB cyclists' bikes, nutrition, sleeping patterns, etc. resulted in an array of medals that was the envy of the world. The exercises will therefore ask of you only what is achievable. For example, 'Today, I want you to do nothing more than listen.' This bite-sized chunk is a stepping stone to the next change. You don't have to do everything at once.

There's no such thing as failure

When families are going through a rocky patch, many parents despair and feel that they have failed at parenting. But when your kids yell and answer back, although the feedback might be negative, it's still only an opinion. At times like these, it's worth adopting Thomas Edison's robust take on such situations, which was that he had not failed — he'd simply not yet found the right way of achieving what he was after. Try reframing the word 'fail' with this handy mnemonic:

First
Attempts
In
Learning

Viewed this way, failure is part of success. So if you try something in these exercises and it doesn't work as planned, you haven't failed. Just accept that some things work for some people and not for others, and try something else.

Screw it – just do it!

That's the Richard Branson approach. You can't really 'try' to do something. You either commit to it or you don't. The word 'try' paves the way for a less-than-wholehearted approach. It provides a get-out clause if things aren't going to plan — which they are far more likely to do with limited momentum behind them. It's amazing what you can achieve if you don't know something's meant to be difficult, so rip off the Band-Aid and get on with it.

Chapter 2

Introducing the Role Model Matrix

To change bad habits, we must study the habits of successful role models.

——————————— *Jack Canfield* ———

The Role Model Matrix is a five-part framework to help you think about the changes you want to make and how you're going to approach taking action. This framework is made up of the following elements:

(M) = Mindset

(O) = Obstacles

(D) = Dynamics

(E) = Emotions

(L) = Language

I suggest that you examine the elements in this order, as a complete package, although you could use them independently. For example, if your main concern was simply improving your conversations with your child, you might want to focus only on the language element of the model.

It's intended as a tool for parents and carers, but if you see results from it, feel free to share it with your child and use it as a basis for discussions.

Defining the model

The next five chapters will examine each element in great detail; the following are brief descriptions of each.

Mindset

How you view a situation is a result of your mindset. It may be something of a personal-development challenge to scrutinise your mindset and establish exactly what it is that you're 'bringing to the party'. What is your agenda? Are you bringing any emotional baggage into the situation, perhaps despite yourself? It's important to understand your mindset before setting about making a change so that you can be resilient, and confident that your approach is based on reasoned decisions rather than emotional reactions.

Obstacles

You need to know what you're up against. Why haven't you achieved a harmonious family life, if that's what you're after? The reasons could be external, such as your child's using drugs or having problems at school, or internal, such as tensions in relationships with your own parents or unhelpful patterns of behaviour shaped by earlier events in your life and triggered at crisis points. These are the things that are holding you back, standing in the way of effective communication, and blocking constructive emotions.

Dynamics

For good or ill, there is a pecking order in every family, and each member occupies their specific roles, whether they are aware of it or not. The makeup of the family very much determines how it operates as a unit. For example, who the resident adults are, and the number of children will certainly have an impact on the relationships between each individual. Evolving families – with the introduction of step-parents / step-children also require inevitable adjustments. The equilibrium within a family can be affected by what one of its members is bringing in from the outside — conflict often occurs when teenagers assert their independence by hanging around with the 'wrong crowd'. All of these issues should be acknowledged, before too much judgement is passed!

Emotions

Emotions are a key part of family dynamics. Understanding how your child is feeling, and how other family members are feeling, is essential — and you must not ignore your own feelings. The adolescent's brain is going through a massive change, and it may be hard for an adult to recapture exactly what the teen is experiencing. Just developing insight into the pressures individuals may be under, and into the sheer biological impact of adolescence, paves the way for greater kindness, to the child and to yourself.

Language

Language, in its widest sense, is how we communicate with one another. Even within a family, people will have very different communication styles, which can sometimes give rise to misunderstandings. The chapter on language will feature exercises on building rapport and on using specific language to help you and your child cut through the faulty assumptions and entrenched positions that can bedevil family life. These exercises are designed for families and parents, but they can be applied just as successfully in the business world or in the social sphere.

Developing the model

I have devised this model on the basis of personal experience: from listening to what clients have said, from what I've heard from teenagers on ChildLine, and from families I've supported through Home-Start. Many parents have said to me, 'I know I'm the one who's supposed to be seeing you, but could you help my son instead?' But to be honest, that's the parents' job. My job is to help them to give that help, and that's why my first port of call is *their* mindset. As the captain of the ship, they need to know how to steer it. I use a journey as a metaphor: if you want to get from A to B, B being your 'brighter future' and A being 'here' and now, you need to know where 'here' is; you need to know where you currently stand.

When parents present an 'awkward' child to me, usually there's a problem that goes a bit deeper than 'wayward teenager'. That's why I examine the whole family environment and the parents who are its linchpin, rather than just looking at the child in isolation. If adults don't accept the need for change and take responsibility, how on earth can they expect their children to do the same?

Through the practice of NLP, I've accepted that we all carry emotional baggage around with us, and that it may not be helpful to go raking over the past. Instead, I encourage parents to look forward rather than back, enabling them to make a new start.

The challenge of change

My view, as set out in Chapter 1, is that it's the adult's responsibility to initiate change, and this is implicit in the term 'role model'. I couldn't put it better than Mahatma Gandhi: 'Be the change you wish to see in the world.' Your overt willingness to change and openness in reaching out to your child will provide powerful evidence of your positive intentions.

When we become parents, we're not given an instruction manual. (We're not given one for life in general, come to that.) Now that families are often dispersed across the country or the globe, and not living together in communities, there's less continuity. If you're a young mum living a long way from parental support, you can feel very isolated and lacking in confidence about what you're doing. What this book aims to do is help you navigate some of the problems that I see come up time and again, in families of all shapes and sizes.

Taking up the challenge of change is vital work; after all, families are the place where people are made.

Chapter 3

Mindset

" ————————————————————————

*You have brains in your head. You have feet in
your shoes. You can steer yourself any direction
you choose.*

———————————————————— *Dr Seuss* ————

The point of departure

Do the battles raging in your house leave you feeling
exhausted? Once you've acknowledged the pain that you,
and maybe others in your family, are going through, doing
nothing is not an option: you'll be stuck with the same old
arguments, the same lack of respect, and the same col-
lection of unhappy people living together under one roof.
You know that something has got to change, but you're just
not sure what it is. Clearly, your current thinking and con-
sequent behaviour aren't producing the results you want.

You need to change to get rid of all that; to have more
freedom to have fun as a family; to understand and accept
one another; to have better relationships; to have more
trust; and to feel more relaxed.

Rewiring your thinking

To limber up and flex your thinking to allow for the possibility of change, try this simple exercise: think of your postcode, and then think of it backwards. It probably comes to mind instantly in the correct order, but to say it backwards, you have to slow down and concentrate. Because you're not used to thinking of it in this way, start by reversing just the second part of it and saying it to yourself a few times until it trips off your tongue. Then move on to the first part and repeat that until it's coming out smoothly. Now join the two parts.

Have you got it? Now move on to your mobile number!

Apart from opening up your mind to viewing things from a different perspective, what this exercise demonstrates admirably is that

- all it takes is a little bit of practice to master a task, and

- breaking a task down into smaller parts makes it achievable.

Both of these are valuable tips for all the exercises in this book — and, not least, will serve as the basis for making any changes in your life.

In order to take charge and steer this ship to a brighter future, you need to understand your current position; you need to know what you stand for and what you want your family to stand for and set a course for it. There is work to do, but by following the process, you will emerge into a future where your pleasure in your family and in your relationships with its members reasserts itself.

The process is based on two Cs: clarity and core values.

Ⓒlarity

Understanding where you are at this moment does not entail beating yourself on the breast over your perceived failures.

❌ 'I'm a hopeless parent and everything's falling apart!'

✔️ 'I'm exactly where I need to be right now.'

The most important thing to do is to accept your current reality without apportioning blame. There might be forgiveness involved, of yourself and of others.

It is vital to pinpoint the source of your problems and keep them in perspective. Overreacting is what is threatening to send you off course, rather than any serious shortcomings as a parent or a person. To redress the balance, take a few minutes to complete this simple exercise.

I'm pretty good, really!

Celebrate your successes by listing three or four achievements you're proud of. For example:

⚙ successes in the workplace

⚙ creative output in leisure activities

⚙ sporting achievements

⚙ sensitive handling of delicate family situations

Think about what factors contributed to those achievements.

Now look at things in your life that made or make you feel happy or fulfilled:

✿ having relationships (spouse, friends, etc.)

✿ taking a stand about something

✿ getting out of your comfort zone, and coping well with it

Again, try to identify the factors that make these aspects of your life so rewarding.

■■■

This is the best antidote to those feelings of hopelessness and helplessness that sometimes threaten to engulf us. Your list will highlight your strengths and give you the confidence that comes from knowing that, actually, you're more than capable. You'll feel happier and more able to tackle whatever is going on.

It's also a great way of identifying what those in the education and employment sectors call 'transferable skills'. You might realise from doing this exercise that when you're at work, you're in fact a skilled negotiator. This is just what's needed when dealing with troubled teens and family tension — you therefore have valuable experience to apply in these situations. Transferable skills developed in the domestic sphere are just as valuable: diplomacy, budgeting, health and safety — you've probably got all these at your fingertips, so remember that next time you're feeling helpless.

To find out which of your skills could do with further development, you might want to consider various aspects of your life separately and give each one a score out of 10. The following wheel of life diagram is only an example. You could increase the number of sections, or change the elements you are assessing, depending on what's important to you.

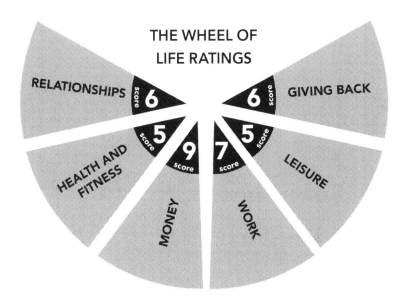

Again, this approach will help you see that some areas of your life are operating perfectly smoothly, and will pinpoint those areas that need a bit more attention. In the example above, the individual has clearly been neglecting health and fitness. The answer for this person would be to invest more time doing active things with family — this would tick three of the boxes!

This information can form the basis for an action plan, so you can carve time out of your schedule for going to the gym, or co-ordinate the family diary to allow for days out together. (And since the topic is non-threatening, it is also a great pretext for a family discussion that demonstrates to children that they have a say and will be listened to.)

Ⓒore values

Once you're clear about your current position, you need to understand your emotional compass in order to recognise the right course of action. It's all very well following your gut instinct, but if you don't know what drives you, what your values and motivators are, there's a danger that you'll head off in the wrong direction, leaving your ship adrift and rudderless.

Imagine you're the coach of a junior football team, and you're keen to get them to the top of the division over the next five games. You could just give them all the standard pep talk, but it wouldn't work in the same way for each of player—because each would be motivated by very different things. What you actually need to know is that one wants to be the next Lionel Messi, another sees the game as a good way of getting out of art class, one wants to make Mum proud, and another plays for the sheer joy of it and doesn't care whether the team wins or loses. Once you're aware of this, you will know what motivators to appeal to when encouraging each individual to give his or her best for the team.

What do I stand for?

Take half an hour, perhaps over a cup of coffee, to reflect on your values, specifically in relation to parenting, the home, and your family as opposed to career and money. The values can be ends in themselves, such as harmony, safety, or growth, or they can be ways of doing things, such as collaboration, patience, or fairness. Jot down as many as come to mind and then, if you want to take it one stage further, prioritise the top five to eight values.

You might realise that harmony, safety, and respect, for example, are way up there at the top but that listening and confidence are way down at the bottom. Recognise those areas that you might need to work on.

[At the back of this book is a list of values that might help you with this exercise.]

■■■

Once people establish their values, they tend to live in accordance with them. In fact, even if they are not particularly conscious of their values, they will still feel uncomfortable when they are doing, or being asked to do, things that don't accord with their values. Once you've worked out what you value the most, you're able to start setting goals. If these goals align with your values, you'll get the end results faster.

Leading the way

Taking care of yourself

Children learn through observing. If we parents constantly put ourselves last, and ignore self-care, what sort of example are we selling for our children? We must understand that as the prime carers of the family, we should be on our own to-do lists. It's nothing to do with selfishness — it's selfish not to take this approach, actually. If we don't look after ourselves and are running on empty, when the vehicle grinds to a halt because we've got nothing left to give, everything else will grind to a halt as well. Put yourself back on the agenda. Just being a bit kinder to yourself will strengthen your confidence in tackling what is going on with your child and redress the balance in family dynamics.

When you are feeling overwhelmed, possibly by the number of challenges ahead – or the extent of a particular obstacle - remember that feeling. That is how your child may well be feeling as well. They're going out into this new world where they don't quite understand the rules yet; they're trying to fit in, but what if they don't? They don't know what's expected of them, and many situations can lead to confusion. By bottling that sensation of feeling overwhelmed, you can empathise with your child.

Involving your child

Only once you've been this through this chapter and started to rebuild the relationship with your child should you think about working with your child on aspects of his or her own mindset. Otherwise, you're likely to get a response along the lines of, 'Listen, I can hardly bear to look at you at the moment, so why would I want to sit down and go through a book with you?' You will be able to judge from the quality of the conversations you are having with your child, and his or her response to initiatives such as, say, family days out, when the time is right to move on from an oblique approach to a more direct one.

Encouraging your child to understand his or her own values is a good place to start. Parents set their children's values up to about the age of seven, after that between the ages of seven and fourteen, children are far more likely to be shaped by peers and teachers, and between fourteen and twenty-one by the wider environment (yes, including the Kardashians!). From adolescence onwards, it's inevitable that their focus moves away from the family, and your visible endorsement and acceptance of this will be a valuable signal for them.

The benefit of helping your child along this route is that, in the future, when you're not around and they have to make hard decisions, these decisions will be a lot easier to make if they — consciously or unconsciously — know what they stand for.

Chapter 4

Obstacles

The only thing standing between you and your goal is the bullshit story you keep telling yourself as to why you can't achieve it.

— *Jordan Belfort*

All you need to do is find the internal blocks and the external blocks, and remove them. It's as simple as that! If only …

Many things can appear to be preventing us from achieving what we want to achieve. It's convenient to cite these things as excuses or even valid reasons for not reaching our goals: 'The economic climate isn't right just now,' 'I'm too fat,' 'My audience isn't ready for this' — you get the picture. Well-meaning friends and family will endorse and commiserate with you, but I'm going to call you out. I have used all these sorts of excuses myself, and I can tell you that they are rubbish.

You can do nothing about the external blocks, such as the economic climate, but you can most definitely do something about the internal blocks.

Internal blocks

The iceberg mind

Think of the mind as an iceberg. The conscious mind is the 4% at the top, the bit that we can see above the water line. It contains all the things we are aware of in the present, such as, 'I should spend more time with the kids,' 'I should set stronger boundaries,' or 'I should give my kids lovely home-cooked meals.' The unconscious mind is the meaty bit: it's the 96%* that supports us. It balances our hormones, reminds us to breathe, tells us to blink, and remembers all the events in our past. It also holds our beliefs, our blind spots, our fears, and our obstacles. It's the unconscious mind that we need to address when we acknowledge our internal blocks.

It is for this reason that I refer this bit of the mind as the UNconscious rather than the SUBconscious. To me 'sub' somehow implies inferiority – where in fact, it is by far the more superior portion of the mind.

The unconscious mind has the best of intentions. It was programmed way back in Neanderthal times to keep us alive and alert to the ever-present danger of sabre-toothed tigers — which are a bit thin on the ground these days. The unconscious mind says, 'I've done really, really well because I've kept you alive until today. Therefore, tomorrow I'm going to do exactly what I did today because it worked.' It's positive thinking, but it's also lazy and safe. We need to push the boundaries a bit to move past the blind spots and the internal blocks, and we can do that by retraining the mind so it works differently.

Most of the beliefs stored in our unconscious mind took root a long time ago, when we were at our most impressionable. Our most clearly defined beliefs were likely laid down before we were six years old. Look at the 'story' of yourself as an infant and small child. What defined your thinking? What is the pattern in conversations you remember? Anyone who has money blocks is likely to have heard recurring variations on a theme in childhood: 'Money doesn't grow on trees,' 'Rich people are greedy and arrogant' — all those sorts of things. As children, we absorb everything like a sponge. If your issue is losing weight, it could go back to the family expectation that you should eat everything on your plate, or to the rule that you could have your pudding only if you'd finished your main course or eaten your greens, or to the exhortation to remember the starving children in Africa and be grateful.

Patterns and stories from our childhood form the limiting beliefs we hold today. We need to address them and challenge them. Acknowledging these beliefs and understanding that you need to change is the first step.

So… What are your issues? What are your stories?

Taking control

Are you your own worst critic? Listen to how you speak to yourself and ask yourself whether you would speak to a five-year-old in the same way. If the answer is 'Definitely not,' stop treating yourself so unkindly then! If you pin down and examine the negative things that your inner voice is saying, you can opt to start doing things differently.

If you let your mind continue to chatter like this, and let the self-doubt continue, you will be doomed to watching your life from the side-lines instead of taking control of it.

The 'I should' Exercise

1. Sit down with your favourite drink and make a long list of all the things that you constantly tell yourself you should do. For example:

✿ I should spend more time with the children.

✿ I should go to the gym.

✿ I should go for a promotion.

✿ I should give up smoking.

There is no limit to the number of 'I shoulds' you can list.

2. Look at your list and ask yourself why you should be doing these things. The answers to this question will both reveal your beliefs and expose your limitations.

3. Change the 'shoulds' to 'coulds' — for example, 'If I really wanted to, I could give up smoking.' Making this mental move gives you a choice.

4. Ask yourself why you haven't made that choice, and you will arrive at the excuses you have been making for yourself.

∎∎∎

Smoking is a classic example of how easy it is to delude yourself about internal blocks. People are perfectly aware of the risks of smoking and the benefits of giving it up, but many still don't want to do it. It may be because smoking is an appetite suppressant and their desire to lose weight wins out over the health risks. It may be because it buys them that short break from their desk or even from their family at regular intervals throughout the day. It's not until you are aware of the real reasons behind a decision that you have an opportunity to make an informed choice.

External blocks

We often start to look for the concrete obstacles standing in the way of a fulfilling family life only when the wheels start to come off. Any parent can reel off a long list of these obstacles, but the following are likely to rank quite highly:

- ⚙ My child has so many extracurricular activities she's doing her homework in the car.

- ⚙ My elderly parents need an increasing amount of my time.

- ⚙ Arguments over 'screen time' are a regular feature of family life.

- ⚙ Microwave meals are taking over because nobody has time to cook.

- ⚙ Time spent together as a family is getting squeezed because I'm working long hours.

To get a handle on all of this, it's useful to sort these external blocks into two categories: environment and people.

Environment

Start by considering the flashpoints in your daily routine. Is it the morning scramble to get everyone up and out?

With young children, it's often bath time or bed time, but with older ones, weekends can be a minefield. Could you make some tiny adjustments that would ease the pressure?

Is your physical environment oppressing you? It's all too easy to drown in the never-ending clutter of family life. Have a look at your workspace. Is your desk chaos? Think how liberating it would be to spend an hour sorting through it and coming away with the huge reward of a workspace you are actually in control of.

Don't be afraid to ask for help with some of this. The British attitude of 'We mustn't grumble and we must keep ourselves to ourselves' could be standing in the way of our making small requests for help that people would be only too happy to agree to (with the possible exception of the teenager in your life!).

Here are some ideas:

- ✿ Arrange reciprocal play dates to free up an afternoon.

- ✿ Create a school-run rota with other parents to ease the pressure on at least one morning a week.

- ✿ Delegate tasks to other family members — you don't have to do it all, and it doesn't have to be done perfectly. (I enlisted the help of my teenagers to clear out my attic, and it almost literally took a weight off my mind!)

Studies show that when children have chores, they gain an understanding and appreciation for responsibility and start developing organisational skills.

People

I hate to say it, but the other thing that could be draining your energy is the people around you. I reckon there are two sorts of people: drainers and radiators.

The drainers are the people who pull you down, the ones who always have something to moan about. They're the people who have drama that they feel duty-bound to offload onto you. They are constantly in 'send' rather than 'receive' mode, so there's little hope that they will ever listen to you and your problems and offer support.

Then there are the radiators, the people who you lift you up, encourage you, support you — I call them the 'can doers'. They are positive thinkers who look for opportunities in place of challenges. It's important to surround yourself with people who will help you if you are brave enough to ask for help.

And then there are your nearest and dearest. While you are making changes, the people closest to you might need time to catch up; they probably won't understand what in the world is going on. These people may be very positive about the changes you're making, but some might regard them as a threat. It's up to you to decide the best course of action, but be aware that it's going to have ripple effects on those closest to you. With patience and gentle persistence, you'll be able to put yourself in their shoes and be sympathetic to their feelings.

Removing external blocks with the three As

You need a strategy to remove obstacles, and this exercise is based on three As.

Advise. Once you've identified what needs to change, communicate your intentions to people. This might involve telling your teenager there are new homework rules, making it clear to your partner that they will be expected to cook a meal three times a week, or notifying your boss that you will be leaving at 5:00 pm at least one day a week. It will be helpful for those affected by the change to know beforehand, so that there are no surprises. Establishing the ground rules early on helps to avoid potential misunderstandings.

Appoint people to help you: a gardener, someone to do the ironing, your best mate to do two of the school runs, a virtual assistant, or a cleaner — whatever works for you. If you can afford to pay for support, do so; if not, build up your support network. (And don't forget that you could and should delegate some tasks to your children. Being a family means pulling together.)

Allow them to get on it with it, whatever 'it' is!

●●●

If your internal and external blocks are stopping you, and you're just staggering from day to day, what sort of example are you setting for your kids? It's all very well saying, 'My child's not working hard enough,' or 'My child's not excelling,' but you need to make sure you're not asking of them something that you're not asking of yourself. Are you walking the talk? Because if not, you can't be a role model. As we know, children learn from observation.

Chapter 5

Dynamics

"

Spend time with those you love. One of these days you will say either "I wish I had" or "I am glad I did".

— Anon —

A family is composed of a number of separate but connected people. Each member has a different personality, different characteristics, different limitations, and different beliefs. Ideally, all these differences will be held in balance, but there will be times when this equilibrium is disturbed — and the eruption of adolescence onto the scene is likely to be one of those times.

Often the parent comes to me about their 'tricky teenager'. However, one person in pain can fracture the entire family. The differences that held the family together can threaten to tear it apart. It therefore makes more sense to address the family as a whole unit rather than to concentrate on just that 'tricky' individual. Love doesn't necessarily mean total agreement between all family members. Lack of agreement is not a bad thing; it's not a failure in parents. Love is about respecting differences and allowing space in the family for them.

The wisest position that parents can adopt at this stage is to acknowledge that they are never too old to learn and that children can teach them a thing or two.

Family roles

The family structure nowadays is very different from what it used to be. In the 'olden' days, the traditional family was 2 parents and 2.2 kids. Now we have blended families, foster families, single parent families, same-sex parent families, adoptive families...

The way the family operates has also changed dramatically over the past century. To find work, today's parents often have to move away from their extended families and have to cope without the traditional support network. Where parents have chosen to remain single, or have separated from the other parent of their children, the children may become estranged from one parent, through no fault of their own.

None of this need matter if each family member can maintain an open mind and be receptive to the possibility of change as new people enter and leave the family unit and change the balance.

Maintaining the balance

Whatever their internal dynamics, families have myriad new challenges and opportunities that they probably haven't experienced before and are therefore ill-equipped to deal with. Respect for one another's welfare and emotions allows for better understanding within the family. All members must have an acknowledged role within the family, and, crucially, it must be a role they are content with. This may require some negotiation.

Mum, for example, might not be getting on very well with her son — she doesn't understand him because his hormones have suddenly kicked in, and she now relates far better to her nine-year-old daughter and tends to gravitate towards her. What she needs to guard against in this situation is favouritism, so it's important for her to maintain open and constructive communication with all family members.

Flexibility is also needed. Family members, especially the parents and primary carers, must be able to swap roles or adopt parts of another's role.

Labels

Have you fallen into the trap of labelling your child? While labels can sometimes be productive, in my experience they are more of a millstone round the child's neck. In my family, my brother was the sporty one and the clever one — for whatever reason, I felt I didn't seem to be worthy of a label. As a result, I believed I was failing to register on my parents' radar. On the flip side, imagine the pressure my brother was under. He lost confidence because he doubted his ability to live up to his labels.

And if that is the effect of positive labels, imagine the impact of negative ones, such as 'the loud one,' or 'the angry one'.

Though they are rarely assigned with any intention of malice, labels can put unnecessary demands on children.

Model behaviour

Children learn from observation. They adopt their family's values and mannerisms at an early age, even though they might later rebel against them. Remember that they will pick up on and probably mirror the way you behave. If you identify problems in your child, you may actually be unearthing a deep-rooted issue that is your own, or another family member's. It might be an issue of authority, money, sex, or power. It's worth taking a step back and questioning from where in the family unit this issue is coming from.

It can also be hard for family members not to pick up on the energy transmitted by others. It's a bit like standing next to someone who is smoking: your clothes absorb the smell of smoke. Energy within the family works in the same way. It may help if you anticipate who is likely to be in what mood at certain parts of the day, and plan and respond accordingly. It doesn't take very many flashpoints to upset the equilibrium of the family. If it feels as though I'm asking you to tiptoe round your family's sensibilities, I would argue that what you're actually doing is taking control.

Remember E+R=O ? Nevertheless, the whole family has got to be involved. You cannot designate one person as having the problem; the whole family benefits if they move forward together.

Make time

Most parents would give their children the shirts off their backs, so the question is, why is it so hard to give them your time? One father said to me that he'd spent most of his adult life working all hours to provide for his family and give them the lifestyle he thought they deserved. At age fifty-five, he took his foot off the pedal a bit to spend more time with his children. Sadly, by then, they had got used to doing without him and weren't really interested: 'No thanks, Dad, I'm fine. We really don't need to go fishing.'

Tomorrow is never promised to anyone, so it's important to start making that time sooner rather than later. Don't wait to start building your relationship with your children. Kids want time now; they don't want money and they don't want procrastination. Look for opportunities to create this time within the everyday family routine. Here are a few ideas, though I'm sure you'll be able to come up with plenty of your own:

- ✿ Let your child teach you how to play a game on the Xbox or PlayStation. They will have your undivided attention, and the added bonus of confidence in knowing more about something than you do.

- ✿ Institute an informal routine that all family members will enjoy — for example, Friday night is pizza & movie night — and stick to it.

- ✿ Conversely, break out of family routine every so often, for, say, a walk somewhere away from your usual environment.

These are ways of creating shared memories. If you can generate some laughter along the way, so much the better: the power of laughter is phenomenal for bonding. And when a family feels that bond, everyone understands that, "OK, we're all muddling along — sometimes we get things right and sometimes we don't — but we're always there for one another." Deep down, love knows how to forgive and how to respect.

Paying attention

More often than not, children, including teens, misbehave as a way of getting their parents' attention. Even though they may not be aware of it, they find any attention, even bad attention, better than none at all. To head this off at the pass, spend one-to-one time with each child. This is so important. What you actually choose to do, whether it's going to a movie, cleaning out the hamster cage, pressing flowers, or playing a few holes of golf, matters far less than the fact that you're actually doing it. I advise making that time at least once a week — and more often if possible, though it depends on how many parents and children are involved, and on their current circumstances — *for a minimum of thirty minutes.*

The main benefit of this approach is that it raises children's self-esteem: they feel loved, they feel that the parent is showing an interest in them and their activities, and they feel valued. It fulfils our three basic needs: that is, our need for respect, for love, and for understanding.

The Teen Blueprint

To restore the family to its well-oiled operations notwithstanding the onslaught of adolescence, here are my tried-and-tested tips.

PROBLEM	TRY TO DO THIS	TRY TO AVOID THIS
My teen doesn't want to talk	✿ Show support and listen ✿ Let her know you are there for her; this helps to build confidence	✿ Constantly asking questions ✿ Appearing desperate for information
My teen keeps answering back	✿ Clarify what he means; this helps to show him that you respect his point of view ✿ If he is being unreasonable, ask for the same respect you're giving him	✿ Getting into arguments; he likely won't be open to your reasoning ✿ Ignoring what he is trying to tell you
My teen keeps making bad decisions	✿ Discuss the situation ✿ Give her opportunities to think for herself ✿ Judge the action and not the child	✿ Punishing her; she is not likely to learn from this
My teen overreacts all the time; everything is such a big deal	✿ Listen ✿ Acknowledge his emotions and try to empathise ✿ Encourage him to deal with the emotional rollercoaster by helping him develop coping strategies	✿ Using critical language: 'You're always so angry' ✿ Telling him to calm down

PROBLEM	TRY TO DO THIS	TRY TO AVOID THIS
My teen spends every spare minute in bed	✿ Remember that teen minds NEED the rest — it's a biological fact ✿ Adopt a relaxed approach to sleep at the weekend and during holidays	✿ Enforcing unrealistic sleep patterns (bear in mind that getting up for school severely disrupts a teen's sleep patterns)
My teen has turned from a sweet child to a strong-willed tyrant	✿ She is trying to exert her independence — encourage this ✿ Give guidance and help her consider her options ✿ Help her understand that actions have consequences; this encourages her to become a good decision maker	✿ Telling her what to do — she probably won't listen ✿ Being inflexible about rules
My teen is so lazy	✿ Think of the long game — this is a phase that will pass ✿ Maintain your equanimity and a resolutely positive approach to him	✿ Picking your battles unwisely ✿ Setting unrealistic expectations
My teen keeps getting into trouble	✿ Allow her to fail — as long as it's safe to do so; this is how teens learn ✿ Ensure she takes responsibility	✿ Lecturing her ✿ Bailing her out — it's not a kindness in the long run ✿ Punishing her if the lesson has already been a hard one — use your judgement

PROBLEM	TRY TO DO THIS	TRY TO AVOID THIS
My teen is experimenting with drugs/drink/ smoking / sex	✿ Get as much knowledge of what is happening as you can ✿ Help him understand his values and long-term goals — he will be more likely to consider the consequences of making foolish decisions	✿ Forbidding him to drink, take drugs, etc. — it won't work ✿ Lecturing him, for the same reason ✿ Not practising what you preach — kids mirror what they see
My teen is being influenced by a bad crowd	✿ Tread carefully — her friends are very important to her ✿ Draw up a 'rescue plan' for if she gets out of her depth; this will reassure her that you're there for her	✿ Disapproving of her ✿ Always believing her Is she is passing the buck? She has to take responsibility

Remember — consistency is essential!

Chapter 6

Emotions

If you want to change the world, go home and love your family.

— Mother Theresa

The overwhelmingly positive emotion we associate with families is love. Although it may not make sense in a practical way, once our need to be loved is met, everything else falls into place. When we are loved, we feel connected, accepted, and happy. Of course there are other positive emotions in the family, but love is the big one.

The big five negative emotions in families are anger, sadness, fear, hurt, and guilt. They come in all shapes and sizes — e.g., you can be frustrated and annoyed — but they fall under the umbrella of these five emotions. We are wired to experience them, and I believe they're not bad.

They're there to protect us, to warn us. They're necessary. When people say we should stamp out negative emotions, I disagree. Admittedly, problems arise when the negative emotions are too dominant because then they start upsetting the family's equilibrium. But also, problems occur when we try to stifle these negative emotions; it's just not healthy. We should educate kids to understand that negative emotions are OK, and we should give them space to deal with them. (We'll be taking a closer look at them in Chapter 11.)

Back to love. There are two types of love, and it's only when we dig deep that we realise that not all love is productive. We've got two types: conditional and unconditional. The question is, what's the difference?

Conditional love

Conditional love is where your concern for another person's well-being and happiness only applies when these are tied in with what you want as well.

The problem is that, as parents, we tend to display a lot of conditional love. We might think, 'I'm different. I must be displaying unconditional love because I love my kids so much and they mean the world to me,' but it's not always the case. We are loving, but I think we're also capable of giving the child the wrong message. A couple of parents said to me recently, 'How does my teen know that I love them when I keep on saying no?' If the child feels unconditional love, your saying no doesn't matter.

Consider this example based on that perennial bone of contention in families: the untidy bedroom. You ask your children to tidy their rooms and when they do, you shower them with praise. They have, in effect, passed the test. If they don't tidy up, you roll your eyes, you signal your disapproval, you nag. Worse still, you might rant and shout and get angry.

Case study: Get a grip!

The mother of two teenagers admitted to me that she constantly cleaned their rooms and made their beds every day. When I asked her why, she said, 'The messy room just drives me crazy! If I didn't do it, I'd just end up shouting at them.'

One viewpoint is that if messy rooms don't bother the teens, it shouldn't bother the parent so much (so long as it's not a health hazard!). Their rooms are their sanctuary, where their rules (within reason) apply. If they have to use wet towels for the fourth day in a row, so be it. This will teach them that it's preferable to hang them out (far more effectively) than if you did it for them all the time.

I then asked her what she would say to her kids if she shouted at them. Her reply: 'God, you never listen to me. Why isn't your room tidy? It's a wreck! You're always so lazy; why do I have to do everything around here?' A clear message of conditional love — and blatant character assassination!

There is, however, the other side of the coin: 'My kids have enough on their plate, so I just want to make their lives a little easier. I'll help them keep their sanctuary more habitable.'

The trick is to adopt the approach that suits you best — while being aware of the messages that you are inadvertently sending to your children.

As far as your children are concerned, you accept them when they're good but not when they're bad. And this type of thinking starts well before the bedroom battles. Very young children do not have the capacity to distinguish between acceptance of them as people and acceptance — or, as the case may be, rejection — of their behaviour. Their simple reasoning will lead them to conclude, 'When I do well, I'm loved; when I do badly, I'm loved less, or I'm not loved at all.'

Breaking the cycle

Young teens lack the emotional maturity to understand that their parents still love them even when they don't like some aspects of their behaviour. If they take personally the anger and antagonism intended for their behaviour, they can start to withdraw and to give up the effort of trying to remain in your favour. This makes them feel isolated, which then makes them feel unloved, and even fearful.

To make matters worse, if they feel isolated, they may find that bad behaviour is the quickest way to get parental attention, if only for a little while. That creates a vicious cycle of bad behaviour, irritation, punishment, withdrawal, isolation, and fear. It's vital to nip that cycle in the bud. I know how tempting it is to send a younger child to his room, or to tell an older one to go away because you can't bear to look at her at that moment. And there you have it, withdrawal rather than an attempt to work things out. But framing this withdrawal in a more positive way — 'We need time out; we need to create space' — can be a constructive approach to take with an older teenager.

What's important is that your children know you are on their side. It doesn't matter whether they've got a detention, been caught smoking behind the bike sheds, or made their girlfriend pregnant — they need to feel confident that you will support them, even if they know you can't condone their behaviour. They need to understand the boundaries and that transgressing them will have consequences but feel secure in the knowledge that your love for them as individuals will not be compromised.

To break the cycle we need to recognise what bad behaviour is and understand what is going on. If you get really angry because they haven't met their curfew, or because they're using drugs or getting bad marks, you're just reacting to the behaviour, which is like reacting to the symptoms and not the cause. It helps to look more closely at the nature of the bad behaviour. Bear in mind that there may well be a distinction between behaviour that you consider bad simply because you find it annoying and behaviour that signifies something more serious. So what's the problem? Is it bad grades? Is it tantrums? Is it lack of communication? Is it the fact that they stay in their room all the time? Are they picking on their siblings?

Find out what's really going on. Family life is never going to be like *The Waltons*. Why is one child out joyriding and another studying hard in the hope of getting straight As? What's missing for the child who's giving you grief? This is when you need to slow down, spend time with your grumpy teen, listen, understand, and reassure. Revisiting his or her purpose and values at this point can also be tremendously helpful. Just try to have these conversations as early as possible, before the wheels come off completely and the child has got used to not speaking to you.

Good boss/bad boss

It's crucial to get these conversations off to the right start. Imagine an equivalent situation in the workplace. Suppose you didn't get a report in on time. Your boss could respond in two ways:

BAD BOSS	GOOD BOSS
That's bloody awful! We've lost a contract because of you. You can't do anything right. That's the last time I give you that responsibility!	What was the problem? Didn't you have the right information? Was the deadline too tight? How could we help you next time? Do you need some more assistance?

Which approach is going to be more productive? Our natural instinct is to reward good behaviour and punish bad behaviour. But in the example above, the resentment and loss of confidence resulting from the first approach could easily pave the way for a vicious circle of poor performance in the workplace. The second approach is far more likely to make you feel supported and understood, and therefore motivated to give your best next time.

How could you apply the good boss approach to the next run-in with your teen?

■■■

Much of the time it's a matter of putting your ego to one side, of ignoring the part of you that just wants to yell at your child to teach her a lesson. It's all too easy to reproduce patterns of behaviour from our own childhoods, even though these could be what get us into our current unsatisfactory circumstances.

Unconditional love

In a nutshell, unconditional love is placing another person's happiness above personal gain and your own needs. It is love – without condtions.

Lasting impressions

Suppose you and I met and spent ten minutes together and for the first nine minutes I was charming, witty, and complimentary about you and your intellect, skills, etc., but for the last minute I was sneering, abusive, foul-mouthed and deeply insulting. What impression would you carry away from the meeting? I bet the horror of the last minute would completely obliterate the previous nine.

That's the thing to consider in your dealings with your children. What's the lasting impression you're leaving them with? Because you can be sure that the nagging grouch will supplant the warm, caring, funny parent if you've fallen into the habit of calling them out for anything and everything. Parents have said to me, 'If I don't shout at my children, they'll think I've gone soft. They'll think they can get away with anything.' Well, better that than that they should think they have forfeited your love. Sometimes the best way to cut through yet another pointless row is just to say, 'Oh, shut up and give me a hug!' You'd be surprised how disarming that can be.

What's the agenda?

A significant problem for teenagers is that they tend to be rewarded only for good behaviour, and this message comes from all angles. It comes from teachers, parents, bosses, and friends. It's about fitting in; it's about knowing the rules, and, more importantly, buying into them. Praise is only given when the recipient is doing what the praise-giver wants. Whilst I am not suggesting you should reward bad behaviour, approaching these misdemeanours with some compassion and understanding might help your child make more informed decisions next time around.

Praise, therefore, is a very subtle form of control. It's fine in the right context, but we need to be careful how we use it in the family. What follows from conditional praise is the perception that love is also conditional. Far better to give some finely tuned attention and some respect, which will signal to children that you are starting to treat them as adults. Here is an approach based on two Cs.

Ⓒlarity

Be clear about what you want. Does your ambition extend only as far as having a child with a tidy room? I doubt it. My guess is that you want your child to be happy and relaxed in a happy and relaxed family, or you wouldn't have picked up this book in the first place. Direct your efforts at maintaining, or perhaps restoring, that open and affectionate relationship with your child rather than ensuring every last sock is off the floor.

Ⓒonsistency

We all like to know where we stand. When teens are going through bewildering changes they cannot control, it's important that home is a place of stability and safety for them. It can be quite frightening to push against boundaries and never meet any resistance, which leads some teens to test them to the point of excess. This is where discussing values can be valuable, as it offers the scope for accommodation on both sides. If you can agree that in the grand scheme of things an untidy room or outlandish clothing matter less than kindness to siblings and the offer of a helping hand around the house, you acknowledge their growing independence and your loving acceptance of it.

Instead of following well-established but scarcely tried-and-tested patterns, we need to think more deeply about ourselves and the relationships we want within our family. We need to feel confident and positive in ourselves so that our happiness is not dependent on a teen's tidy bedroom and our self-esteem is not threatened by a grunt or snarl. Ridding yourself of your ego while not turning into a doormat is the balancing act you must achieve!

You might have to sacrifice your pride for their happiness. Suck it up! It's your job. You're the parent; you're the adult in this situation, so it's your responsibility.

Chapter 7

Language

Communication to a relationship is like oxygen to life — without it, it dies.

Tony Gaskins

The thing about language is that it's not just what you say. Many of the messages that pass between members of a family are wordless: the eye roll, the exasperated sigh, the 'whatever' shrug. The meanings of these messages are unmistakable. As parents, it's assumed that we know how to deploy all communication effectively, and nothing could be further from the truth. If we are not taught how to communicate well, it's no surprise that at times we are misinterpreted.

Good communication is therefore not only about our message, but also about how it's heard. Communication is also about listening — really listening, not just waiting for the moment when you can seize the opportunity to speak. Good communication forms the basis of effective relationships, so it's a skill that needs to be developed.

Look at any organisation, be it a small one like a work team or a large one like a school or a company, and you'll see that the leadership sets the tone of the communication across the organisation. **As leader of your family, it's up to you to set an example by communicating well. One of the most effective ways to become a better communicator is to become a better listener.**

Listen and learn

If a company is failing, management might talk to the people at the grassroots level, to get their opinion on how things could improve. It's no different with families.

And when you're gathering these opinions, listen not only to the words being uttered, but also to the tone of voice. As well, observe body language. So many signals that people send out are non-verbal. And if you get the chance, observe the non-verbal cues of any wider group participating in the conversation.

To listen better, the trick is to ask open-ended questions — those that require more than a monosyllabic reply. You're aiming to invite the speaker to elaborate. If you ask, 'Are you okay?' you'll get a 'Yeah' or a 'No'. If you say, 'Tell me about how you're feeling,' you open up the conversation (though some teenagers may still just shrug), you allow the speaker to go into more detail, and you're able to keep the conversation going with follow-up questions.

Reflecting

1. Ask: What is this child trying to tell me? It might be his or her opinion or version of the truth, but what's the underlying message?

2. Watch: Pay attention to more than just the words. Notice body language, tonality, speed, and degree of emotion.

3. Repeat: State your understanding of what's been said. If we're in a hurry, we're likely to jump to conclusions. We need to stop and hear what's being said. Then we need to repeat what we have heard.

4. Clarify: Ensure your understanding is correct. This shows you appreciate the speaker's situation or recognise how they're feeling.

Teens will tell you if you're on the right wavelength, and if you've misunderstood, they'll certainly let you know. What they're going through might seem insignificant to us, but to them, it's massive. Reflecting what's going through their heads in your conversation shows that you actually listened and that you understand what they're trying to say to you, which will lead to a better conversation. Your child will feel heard and valued.

●●●

I've learned from my involvement with ChildLine that being listened to raises children's self-esteem. So many of the young children say, 'You've made me feel so much better, thanks for listening.' In reality, there wasn't a great deal that needed sorting out. All they needed was somebody to listen, to make them feel understood and respected.

And it's not just the younger generation who feels mis-understood. For every teenager who says, 'My mum just doesn't get me,' there's a parent saying, 'I don't under-stand it, I'm just not on his wavelength. I don't get it.' If this situation arose in a business context, we would sit down and have a different kind of conversation with someone. Well, we need to do the same with our kids, and tailor our approach for each individual child. Some people require a lot of reassurance and empathy, whilst others require a more practical approach and need to discuss the different options available to them. My daughter and son were so different from each other, I had to learn how to speak to them differently to keep the conversation going.

It helps, of course, if you've been paying attention from the beginning. If you haven't been listening to the small stuff — about how they got a star for their colouring, or how they scored a goal in a game, or what their favourite pizza topping is — why on earth would your child think that you're going to be interested in listening to the important stuff, like relationships or peer pressure?

Assuming you're receiving on all channels, and commu-nication is flowing, your next challenge is responding to the stuff that might be difficult to hear (be it drink, play-ing hooky from school or bullying). How you respond will affect how your child behaves in the future. If we don't like what we hear, there's a temptation to shut down and refuse to engage with the situation, perhaps by simply issuing an edict. It's far better to take it on board and adopt a constructive approach to resolving it, preferably with input from the child.

Sometimes we just need to listen better and not make assumptions. All too often parents ask me, 'How do I get through to them? They just don't listen.' Listening should be a reciprocal activity. As parents we're used to being the ones who know how to sort things out, so it's all too easy for us to default to problem-solving mode rather than really listening to the problem.

Talking to teens

The first thing to do is to offer help, so that they know you've got their backs. That, for the time being, might be enough. That might be all that they want to hear. Sometimes parents say, 'He only talks to me when he wants something.' That's fine, but always be there so that when he does want something, he knows that it's all right to say so.

Remember, it's always worth having conversations about the small stuff, rather than conversations that lead only to ultimatums or confrontations. Find out what they're interested in and talk! After all, this is what we do with other adults. Give them your undivided attention and don't be distracted. It's as simple as that. Leave the chores, turn off the phone; if you absolutely have to, reschedule and explain why. You want them to know that you want to help and that you're prepared to give them your time.

TALKING TO TEENS: SOME DOS AND DON'TS

THEY SAY	DO SAY	DON'T SAY
I've got a problem with my girlfriend/boyfriend/bullying at school/my friend taking drugs.	What are your options here?	I think you need to do this.
Can you lend me £10?	Sure, perhaps you can pay me back when your allowance/pay comes in.	You only ever talk to me when you want something!
You just don't understand me!	Explain to me again what it is I haven't grasped.	I've had enough of this. We're going round in circles.
My sister/brother has been taking stuff from my room again.	When did s/he do it before? What did you say that time? What do you think might work better?	Sort it out between you. I haven't got time for this.

Choose your words

Language is all about the words we use and their intended meaning. If there's a gap in the logic, or an alternative meaning, believe me, teenagers will spot it at a hundred paces. Make sure what you say won't be misinterpreted.

Case study: Say what you mean

My daughter, Alice, and I went out to get our hair done. When my husband saw us, he said, 'Nice hair, Alice.'

Instantly I said, 'Hey, I've had mine done as well. Why is it that you never even mentioned my hair? You never mention my hair!'

Three days later, he came home from work, gave me a kiss, and said, 'Good to see you. You need your roots done.'

Well, that showed me. Clearly I had not been specific enough about the sort of comments on my hair that I wanted to hear!

Most of the time we get by without thinking too deeply about what we're saying, but with teens this will not wash. You will avoid a whole lot of unpleasantness if you take the following precautions.

Avoid generalisations **such as**:

✿ Why is your room always a mess?

✿ You're so lazy.

⚙ You never do your homework on time.

⚙ No one in this house listens to me.

You've got to be specific, otherwise everyone switches off.

Avoid general comparisons:

⚙ 'You should be more polite.' More polite than whom?

⚙ 'She's better than you.' At what?

Words are always open to misinterpretation, but parents say to me, 'They should know what I mean.' It doesn't work like that.

Avoid distortions:

⚙ 'You make me so angry!' Where do I start with this one? The choice to become angry is yours. (Again – remember E+R=O)

Avoid ambiguity:

⚙ 'Mum, can I stay over at Sarah's house?' Don't say, 'We've spoken about this before. I want you back by 10 o'clock.' (Does this mean am. or p.m.?)

Your teenager is more likely to disengage than wait for clarification.

Leading by example

'She's got absolutely no respect for me and her father at all, it's absolutely ridiculous. She's behaving like a child.' I get this a lot. The point is, we expect understanding and respect from our children, but as we know, children learn by observation, so the question is, are they receiving understanding and respect from us?

You have to treat your teens like young adults. Yes, they'll get things wrong, and yes, they'll probably throw things back in your face, but I'm afraid that's what you're there for. Times have changed and we can no longer get away with a 'Do as I say, not as I do' approach. Kids are much savvier now and they can see right through it: 'How does Dad expect me to do what he says when I know how he's been behaving behind so-and-so's back?' We have to set an example for our kids. We need to be accountable for our behaviour as well, because our kids watch everything that we do.

You can start the process of change by speaking to family members one to one and then bringing everyone together in a family meeting to communicate expectations so there are no misunderstandings. Say, 'Listen, we need, as a family, to change our game. I appreciate that we will both need to do stuff differently to make things work.' Ask them what they think of this proposal. Have they any suggestions? Then see how the next couple of weeks unfold, with, ideally, everyone making an effort. Once you get everyone to buy into it, you have a sort of contract that everyone feels committed to, and part of its strength is that it is as binding for the adults as it is for the children.

Be patient, and be kind to yourself and all concerned. Changes take time to bed in, and some people need a little bit more guidance and support than others.

PART II

.

Chapter 8

Building Self-Confidence

Confidence is quiet, insecurities are loud.

Confidence is the issue that people consult me about most often. These are some of the frequent laments I hear from parents:

⚙ Why has her sparkle gone?

⚙ He's stopped seeing his friends.

⚙ She's so hard on herself.

⚙ His self-esteem is at rock-bottom.

The teenagers themselves say things like:

⚙ I just don't feel good enough.

⚙ I don't know what's going on, but I want to stop feeling this bad.

What is confidence?

It's worth distinguishing between self-confidence and self-esteem. Self-confidence is about how you rate your ability to perform particular tasks: driving a car, baking a cake, or sitting an exam, for example. There are plenty of people who, say, don't feel confident public speaking but who have absolute confidence that they can write an elegant report. Self-esteem is about how you value yourself. The trouble is, a low estimation of yourself can lead you to doubt your ability to do things that, from a rational perspective, you are more than capable of performing.

Our self-esteem is part of our belief system, and it colours our unconscious view of ourselves. It often devalues the qualities and abilities we have that could be verified by an objective assessment. These negative beliefs may have been formed when we were very young, as discussed in Chapter 4.

It's all too easy for children to absorb the negative comments fired at them and start developing a poor opinion of themselves. There comes a point when you stop questioning your beliefs and simply accept that they're true. If we don't value ourselves, we don't value what we do. This low self-esteem leads to lack of confidence and impairs the way we function in everyday life. We resist making changes or taking risks for fear of rejection or harsh judgements.

There is a danger, if we don't trust ourselves, that we might simply withdraw. Isolation works against our need for connection, for feeling valued, and once such needs are not met, we are on a slippery slope.

When we feel confident, we're more likely to feel calm and relaxed. This means we feel more in control, so we may start taking risks and even feeling good about ourselves. Studies show that improving our self-esteem and our self-confidence — means we live happier lives. We're more capable of embracing the challenges and taking up the opportunities that life throws at us; we are able to make tough decisions, we have stronger coping strategies, we handle criticism more easily, and we view life more optimistically.

Building confidence

So how can we take control and challenge our unconscious beliefs? The next exercise is a good starting point. And remember, it is a starting point. If you think about how a toddler learns to walk, you'll realise that as adults, we take a very different approach to learning. A toddler doesn't mind how many times she falls down on her bottom — she keeps trying until she succeeds. She wouldn't dream of stopping. As adults we tend to expect an early reward and give up if it looks too hard. Yet falling is part of the learning process; early failure is a part of ultimate success.

Confidence-builder exercise

When we do something that we are good at, we usually feel confident about our abilities. We also feel confident with people we like and who are nice to us. Firstly, write down something that makes you feel confident, or that you are confident about.

What you are going to do is hardwire the feeling you get from that activity or person. In NLP we call this 'anchoring'. An anchor is a physical cue that acts a bit like a trigger — think of pieces of music that for whatever reason make you feel happy or motivated. You're going to set up a conscious trigger, so that whenever you want to feel confident, you can just use this anchor. It's great for the times when you feel a bit nervous, perhaps when you have to give a presentation, or you're in a strange social situation.

1. Establish the anchor

* ⚙ Choose an anchor that you can use anywhere; for example, pulling your earlobe or putting your thumb and index finger together.

* ⚙ Close your eyes and think of a time when you felt calm and relaxed, strong and in control: confident. Picture yourself in that situation right now.

* ⚙ What do you see? What do you hear?

* ⚙ Make that picture in your head bright and colourful. Imagine as much as you can about that event. Whom are you with? What's being said?

* ⚙ Really feel as if you are living the moment. You are as calm and as confident as can be. Let those feelings wash over you.

* ⚙ 'Fire the anchor' — in other words, pull your earlobe or do whatever it is that you've decided your trigger will be.

* ⚙ When that feeling fades, remove the anchor.

2. Break the state

* ⚙ To return to normal, think of something else for moment. Try to remember what you had for breakfast, perhaps.

3. Fire the anchor again

⚙ Repeat Step 1.

⚙ Make the same pictures in your head, with the same sounds and feelings.

⚙ Make them as strong as you can.

⚙ Fire the anchor, and when the feelings fade, remove the anchor.

4. Break the state again

⚙ Return to a neutral state.

5. Fire the anchor once more

⚙ You'll probably find that you can do this quite quickly now. It's just a matter of practice.

•••

The way this exercise works is that the anchor tricks the unconscious mind into feeling confident. Confronted with the repetition, the unconscious mind says to itself, 'Oh, OK, this is happening again and again and again, so I know what I'm doing, and I'm doing it well.' Every time you repeat the exercise you 'rewire the brain' and strengthen the neural pathways, so that you get used to feeling incredibly confident or capable.

Failure is feedback

The exercise above is useful for adults and teens alike, but as a parent you'll probably want to give your child a hand developing a healthy level of self-confidence. There's no better way of doing this than by setting an example. Let your children see you tackling fresh challenges and developing new skills — and, just as importantly, acknowledging your own anxieties as you do so. It's vital that children see that it's normal to be apprehensive about new things, and that it's part and parcel of the learning process.

We all learn by the trip-and-fall method. By demonstrating this to your kids, you send the message that it's safe for them to learn and to test new things (though you might want to have that conversation about boundaries at some time!) without incurring criticism and negative judgements. It's a lesson that will carry them into adulthood. It will enable them to tackle new things even when they no longer have the safety net of parents on tap.

A preventive attitude is counterproductive on the grounds that 'This is all going to end in tears' because sometimes it has to. Children don't listen to their parents all the time. Learning first-hand that mistakes happen and the world doesn't cave in as a result, is beneficial for their personal growth.

Its worth remembering, that it's fine to be rewarded for your achievements but even better to be rewarded for your efforts. All too easily we focus on the end result, like the exam grade or the final score. Success is not always guaranteed; you can't always be the winner. This is a lesson our children would benefit from learning early on in life. Showing them you value their effort helps to build their resilience, and resilience depends to a degree on appreciating that no effort is ever truly wasted. Even if you fail, you will have acquired new knowledge, developed greater skill, and extended your personal experience in the world. As previously stated – children learn by observation – so you may bear in mind it's worth practising what you preach when tackling your own tasks and challenges!

Passion and planning

One of the most positive things you can do for your child is to help her find her passion and then support her in following it. Remember, her interests might be different from yours. We tried to introduce our son, to every sport that his school had to offer, but he greeted each with a lukewarm response. It wasn't until he got to university that he discovered rowing — a sport that finally grabbed his attention. Not only that, he is now a qualified ski instructor. When given the space, we have the opportunity to find our own path.

Try not to put a dampener on youthful ambitions, even if they don't seem to be pointing in the direction of gainful employment. Countering an aspiration such as 'Mum, I want to be a musician' with, 'That's lovely, dear, but just pass your exams and become an accountant first' will do nothing to enhance your relationship with your child and gives a clear signal that you're more interested in his solvency than his happiness.

A more constructive and realistic approach is to encourage him to plan for the future by setting goals. OK, so he wants to be a musician: What will he need to do aside from becoming proficient at playing his instrument? How can he start making these things happen? Considering these questions will give your child a sense of purpose. So many people in the age bracket of seventeen to twenty-five have no idea what they want to do with their lives, but once they work it out, it can be transformational.

Give yourself a gong

Don't be so focused on the goal up ahead that you forget to celebrate what you're achieving along the way; like the child at Christmas who gets so engrossed in the process of opening presents that he doesn't look at what each one is before moving on to the next one. Encourage children and teens to take a pride in what they have achieved, and remind them of any accomplishments they may have over-looked. Help them understand that progress and bolster their sense of their capabilities.

To adopt this constructive approach, you must reject per-fection. It's not realistic; it's inhibiting. Despair in the face of perfection is what discourages people from even trying to pursue their passions. Encourage your teens to embrace all their idiosyncrasies, and demonstrate to them that this is your own approach to life.

CONFIDENCE CHECKLIST

✿ Keep learning new things.

✿ View failure as feedback.

✿ Learn from mistakes.

✿ Reward effort.

✿ Find your passion.

✿ Have a plan.

✿ Celebrate success.

✿ Avoid perfectionism.

✿ Last but not least, and underpinning everything else, give unconditional love.

Chapter 9

Coping with the Lies

I'm not upset that you lied to me; I'm upset that from now on I can't believe you.

— *Friedrich Nietzsche*

It is claimed by researchers at the universities of Ghent, Vanderbilt, Amsterdam and Maastricht, that 75% of adolescents lie. "Around 75 per cent of adolescents lie, with an average of nearly three lies a day, but with 60 per cent telling up to five porkies daily."

So what can we, as parents, do about this?

It can be quite scary when you discover for the first time that your child has been lying to you. I don't mean the blatant 'innocent' lying of a toddler who stands in front of you with their mouth covered in chocolate, swearing blind they haven't pilfered any. I mean a proper, calculated, barefaced lie. But there's no cause for alarm. You can heave a sigh of relief because this is perfectly normal.

Just a word of warning, though. At whatever age you catch your child lying, nip it in the bud. If they realise early that they can get away with it, they'll learn that it's a great way to get out of trouble, and they'll be more likely to lie in the future. As they grow older their lies are likely to get bigger and more serious.

Why children lie

It's important to remember that your child isn't lying to you because they're bad. Children lie because they don't want you to *think* that they're bad. Children learn early that not doing what you want them to do is 'bad'. They're afraid that we, the parents, will withhold our love from them if they're bad, and who can blame them for forming this view? It relates directly to the issue of conditional versus unconditional love discussed in Chapter 6.

There's no getting away from the fact that kids lie. They do so

- ✿ to hide their mistakes;
- ✿ to avoid getting in trouble;
- ✿ to fit in; and
- ✿ to avoid upsetting other people.

Do any of these reasons look familiar to you? Don't be too judgemental because we all lie for exactly the same reasons.

Well, if we're all doing it, is lying actually so bad? A lie told to protect others from hurt is understandable, and indeed often actively encouraged — pretending to like an ill-chosen present, for example. For young children the distinction between an ordinary lie and a white lie is a fine one, but we need to teach them to be kind with the truth, or at least to choose their words carefully and not be so brutally honest that they end up alienating people. (Though we all need to avoid those killer phrases that seem intended to soften unpalatable truths but are actually freighted with thinly veiled nastiness: 'With respect' and 'Don't take this the wrong way, but… ')

I hear both sides of the story. Parents complain, 'All I hear are endless lies,' and children grumble, 'Mum makes such a fuss if I don't tell the truth.' We parents must remember that lying happens when we're trying to create a better impression and avoid disapproval. It goes back to that inherent need we have to be loved and accepted.

Because of this, what children need to grasp is that we will love them despite their mistakes, and that we don't judge them when they get things wrong. Getting this message across is one thing, but I realise that demonstrating it in day-to-day life may be easier said than done. It is important to try to do so, though.

Throughout this book I suggest laying out the ground rules early and discussing the consequences of breaking them, and this topic is no exception. Research shows that children are more likely to obey the rules if they are agreed to in advance and deemed to be fair. We need to explain to our children that they should tell the truth, no matter how uncomfortable it may make them feel. We must also make sure we take the opportunity to praise them for telling the truth, even if they have owned up to something we may not be happy about. Make a clear distinction between the offence and their bravery in having come clean.

Lying to conceal the truth is a problem when

- ✿ it develops into a repeating pattern;
- ✿ it constitutes a threat to safety; and
- ✿ it is based on feeling accepted (within a peer group, for example).

WHAT DO KIDS LIE ABOUT?

Anything and nothing:

- ✿ Whether they did their homework
- ✿ Whom they're visit after school
- ✿ Who hit whom first
- ✿ Whom they're hanging out with
- ✿ Whether they've started dating
- ✿ Whether they've had a cigarette
- ✿ Whether a party is supervised
- ✿ Where they're going

Interestingly, research from Nancy Darling's Lab, Psychology Department at Oberlin College, has shown that in families where there is less lying, there are more likely to be arguments or complaints. This suggests that children who feel comfortable with negotiation and dissent feel less need to lie. And we know that children who feel comfortable talking openly and honestly to their parents have greater self-confidence and self-esteem.

Denying mistakes and dodging the blame

When children lie to hide the mistakes they've made, they're not taking responsibility and not learning the lessons that will equip them for the future. They will possibly, keep on making the same mistakes.

You can help them be more willing to own up to slip-ups by not blowing these errors in judgement out of all proportion. Make sure you're not, either overtly or covertly, sending out the message that failure is shameful and to be avoided, otherwise you'll encourage them to conceal or deny these errors. If you can present failure and mistakes as opportunities for learning, then coming clean won't be such an ordeal.

As a parent, it helps to be able to distinguish between genuine mistakes & failures and wilful disobedience & rule breaking. Make sure your child understands how differently you will treat these situations.

And we've all heard these familiar cries: 'She started it!' 'It's not my fault!' If children keep blaming others and never take responsibility, then yet again, they aren't learning. There's a risk that the same things will keep happening.

The lesson we therefore need to teach our children is not that lying leads to punishment, but that it has consequences.

What to do when your children lie

By helping your children learn from their mistakes, you're helping them develop critical thinking skills. Tempting though it is to go ballistic when you catch your children lying, it's not recommended. The following measured approach will be far more constructive in the long run.

Critical thinking model

This model works for any mistakes, problems (e.g., bullying), or errors in judgement (e.g., choice of friends). This approach will better equip your child for future decisions.

The trick is not to

- ✿ give away the answer — they need to process the situation themselves;

- ✿ sort the issue out for them — they need to learn for themselves.

The ability to process a situation with a degree of objectivity and hindsight is much more valuable than outright punishment. However, punishment may also be necessary so that your child will understand that actions do indeed have consequences. You'll know what best works for you and your child.

1. Mind your language

- ✿ Remain calm.

- ✿ Choose your words carefully: flying off the handle will make them defensive (and resolved never to own up to anything or get caught out again).

- ✿ Do not launch into a lecture, as they will not learn from it at this stage.

2. Create a safe place

- ✿ Acknowledge that there is no such thing as failure, only feedback.

- ✿ Reinforce that they are allowed to make mistakes.

- ✿ Encourage them to work out why the mistake, problem, or poor judgement happened.

3. Ask for the truth

- ✿ Explain to them why honesty is important.

- ✿ Listen to them.

- ✿ Do not judge.

- ✿ Do not react — yet.

4. Ensure you've got the full story

- ✿ Establish the facts as best you can.

- ✿ Keep asking open-ended questions.

- ✿ If need be, give them alternatives to telling you what happened (for example, they might want to write it all down, as eye contact can be daunting).

- ✿ Make sure you are really hearing everything that happened.

- ✿ Repeat these steps until you have the full story.

5. Ask for their opinion

- ✿ Establish the cause and effect.

- ✿ Ask them why they think this happened.

✿ Ask them what caused the outcome.

✿ Perhaps establish why they acted in a certain way.

✿ (All these help them to predict future outcomes.)

6. Explore the solutions

✿ Ask them what they would do differently next time.

✿ Discuss what they are going to do to make amends.

✿ Help them think through problems critically.

7. Avoid being judgemental

✿ Work out how you can support them.

✿ Encourage them to articulate what lessons they have learned.

✿ Thank them for their honesty.

■■■

Experience tells me that without this approach, the lying is likely to continue. Children want to be treated like adults, so it's worth giving them the benefit of the doubt and trying out this approach with them. If the lying continues, however, they have forfeited the right to be treated like an adult and the consequences may become harsher.

But be prepared to be flexible, too. Compromise is not a sign of weakness; it doesn't mean that you're backing down. Kids often lie because they can't be bothered to have the war of words with you, so pick your battles carefully and remember that you don't always have to 'win'.

Secrets and lies

For the adult, there is a clear difference between white lies designed to spare people's feelings and secrets that, if harboured for too long, can have a corrosive effect on health and wellbeing.

However for the younger child – they do not have the mental capacity to make that distinction just yet.

Why is honesty so important?

The point is that lies — even tiny fibs that you deem acceptable — can escalate and lead to problems:

✿ inauthenticity (you're not being who you really are);

✿ a power imbalance in relationships (secrets erode trust); and

✿ stress (sustaining big lies can damage your health).

Honesty is therefore not only vital for the emotional well-being of any individual—it's also the cornerstone on which relationships are built. This is why it's worth explaining to your child that lying breaks down the trust between you, and consequently, you'll be reluctant to give them the free rein they're so desperately seeking.

Health and safety

In some cases the truth has to outweigh any other consideration. This is particularly relevant when it comes to issues that may put people's health and safety at risk, such as drink, drugs, sex, violence, smoking, and driving. It's important to discuss the risks with your child in advance, and be very clear that honesty is paramount in these circumstances. In extreme cases, misplaced loyalty to friends or a conspiracy of silence could have fatal consequences.

Where at all possible, do not make your child choose between their loyalty to you and their loyalty to their friends. The peer pressure on them is huge, and if you back them into a corner they might make the wrong decision for them; being excluded from their friendship group could be worse than any punishment from you.

■■■

Lying may well go with the teenage territory, but once the penny drops and they understand that by lying they forfeit their right to be treated as adults, equilibrium should return to the family. Although the ball is well and truly in their court when it comes to lying, it may take teenagers several iterations of the cycle of deceit/discovery/resolution before they fully grasp the concept.

LYING CHECKLIST

✿ Remember that most children lie at some stage; it's quite normal, the reasons being they don't want you to think they're bad.

✿ Don't let your child get away with lying; nip it in the bud.

✿ Encourage open discussion and challenge; there is less lying in families that do so.

✿ Explain to your child that lying erodes trust and makes it less likely that you'll give them the freedom they seek.

✿ Make sure your child understands there is nothing wrong with genuine mistakes and failures.

✿ Applaud your child's bravery if they tell the truth in difficult circumstances.

Chapter 10

Understanding Social Media

I fear the day that technology will surpass our human interaction. The world will have a generation of idiots.

———————— Attributed to *Albert Einstein* ————

When kids are using these devices, using the internet, chatting on Facebook, or playing video games – their brains will remain active – even if they are tired.

Coupled with the fact that the developing brain, in fact, needs more sleep than adults this puts increased stress on our children.

As parents, our ultimate goal is to see our children grow up happy and safe. However, social media can also introduce new pressures for our children – as they strive to measure up to the photo-shopped – celebrity culture that now lands in the palm of their hand on a daily basis. This has made it harder in some ways for parents to achieve this goal; particularly so for those whose own exposure to media amounted to no more than four terrestrial channels and a telephone on the table in the hall.

But we cannot abdicate responsibility and hide behind excuses such as, 'I'm a technophobe,' or 'I hate all that Facebook stuff anyway.' That's a reckless attitude. It's our responsibility as parents to understand the Internet as a whole and how it can affect our children. Technology is not going to go away, and the sooner we're able to guide our children through the minefield the better.

Devices such as computers, tablets and smart phones emit blue light, which tricks the brain into thinking that it is still daytime and that the mind needs to remain awake and alert. This blue light also stops the brain producing melatonin – which is the hormone that regulates our sleep patterns.

We must also aim to ensure that the interactions between our child and the people they communicate with online are safe and constructive. Beyond this, we need to consider why our children are so hell-bent on looking for online approval – from people they have not met in real life – rather than spending quality time with loved ones. For teens, this is partly bound up with the notion of FOMO: fear of missing out. It's all too easy to forget that on sites like Facebook and Instagram, what you're seeing are edited versions of other people's lives. For insecure teens, what they see online may confirm their suspicion that everyone else is more attractive, more popular, more successful and having more fun than they are. Exposure to carefully curated personae on screen has the potential to amplify any germ of self-doubt or low self-esteem.

I wouldn't for a minute dispute the many benefits of the Internet, not least because our son lives in Canada and it's wonderful to be able to interact with him online and know that he's OK. The benefits for business are immeasurable too. The Internet has improved relationships between companies and customers, and has enhanced accountability.

The dangers out in the ether, however, are legion: child grooming, cyber bullying, fraud, sexual harassment, inappropriate content — the list goes on and on. Nobel Peace Prize winner 1921 - Christian Lous Lange, a historian and political scientist, said that 'technology is a useful servant but a dangerous master'.

To keep social media under control and avoid being controlled by it, consider the helpful mnemonic:

(S)ecurity
(A)nonymity
(F)alse environment
(E)verlasting
(T)iming
(Y)ourself

(S)ecurity

Monitoring Internet safety for younger children is the easy bit. Two simple guidelines should do the trick:

 ✿ have a family computer for everyone to use, so you can keep an eye on what the kids are up to; and

 ✿ install filters to ensure that your child is unable to access unsuitable sites.

The problem becomes far more unwieldy once your child has independent access to the web through a phone, a tablet, a laptop, or even a watch. As parents, we have very little influence on the level of device usage, and we simply won't be present for some of the time that our children are online, so monitoring and punishment are not effective options. Once our children get to a certain age, we must educate them instead, so that they're aware of the consequences of the choices they make online.

The topic of security can be summed up by my six Ps: people, personal details, passwords, privacy settings, public WiFi, and prudence.

People

It's important for children to understand that unless they know personally the individual with whom they're interacting online, they must assume that that person has their own agenda. It may not necessarily be a bad agenda, but it's likely to be different from that of your child.

Teach your child that not everyone she comes across online can be trusted as a friend. Girls in particular need to remember that although they might trust their boyfriend enough to 'sext' him, he might then trust a mate, and that mate might then… It wouldn't take long for that picture to reach someone far removed from the sexter who feels no compunction to respect her privacy. (A sext is a sexually explicit message or photograph sent on a mobile phone or other device.)

Personal details

It's not wise to place obvious personal information online — bank details, home address, etc. — but an awful lot of information can be inferred from innocent-seeming posts as well. Tempting though it is to post pictures of your children in uniforms on their first day at school, be it primary or secondary, these photos alert anyone with less than benevolent intentions to your child's location, and possibly gives them clues about your own whereabouts at a particular time of day. As well, you might think twice about posting information to the effect of 'We're going on holiday for the next two weeks', but 'Here we all are having a lovely time on the Golden Gate Bridge' is nearly as harmful.

Passwords

Most younger kids tend to have one password for everything, and that's fine. It's more important to have multiple passwords that you change regularly when dealing with more sensitive areas like internet banking — or when children reach the stage where geeky frenemies may try to hack their social media accounts. If keeping track of it all is beyond you, consider using a password manager app such as LastPass or 1Password.

Privacy settings

Do you know exactly who is viewing your social media posts? And even if you do, it's worth asking yourself, 'Would I care if my grandmother saw this?' or even, 'Would I mind if this was on the front page of tomorrow's *Sun*?' If the answer to both of these questions is no, then carry on. If it's 'OMG! I would just die!' then maybe think about not posting whatever it is. That goes for you and your children.

Lax privacy settings allow for friends of friends to relay things to their friends. The material can swiftly pass to people who are total strangers, so be aware of this. You can amend your privacy settings for each piece of software being used to maintain tighter controls and thus security.

Public wifi

Information can leak through public wifi. (Public places, such as airports and coffee shops, often offer Internet access. Public wifi makes your device vulnerable to hacking.) It's wise to turn off network discovery and file sharing when using public wifi, especially if your device has access to your sensitive information.

Prudence

Be careful what you open and what you click on. Just the other day I was on a trusted site and clicked on something that claimed to link to a survey related to parenting. Instead, I found myself confronted with a lot of ladies who seemed to have forgotten to put their tops on. Also, make sure you warn children about not opening emails from people they don't know. They will probably be the ones to suffer most if your PC or their device succumbs to a virus!

(A)nonymity

Social media is a way of socialising without socialising. People interacting via technology may feel they are joining in, but often they are unwittingly isolating themselves further.

Yet they're not isolating themselves in the safety of four walls. They're isolating themselves, potentially, in the middle of a bunch of complete strangers, in real time — live streaming is accessible and prevalent. The illusion of safety can make it tempting to behave in ways that are inappropriate, but whatever you do will be out there forever.

(F)alse environment

Children look at filtered and often carefully manipulated images of other people's lives. They compare the glorious technicolour world that others seem to inhabit with their own seemingly humdrum, black-and-white surroundings. They're also tricked into feeling that they're in a real community, and a child lacking in confidence may be particularly susceptible to comments such as, 'You look so hot in that picture.' A young girl might think a cute boy made the comment when in fact it was a sleazy forty-five-year-old sitting in his Y-fronts in Arizona (though I'm sure there are perfectly nice, non-sleazy forty-five-year-olds in their underpants in Arizona!). Even if they understand how superficial it is, children may continue to find the virtual world strangely compelling. As one fifteen-year-old said: 'It's a bit like an awkward family dinner that you just can't leave.'

Ⓔverlasting

Teens tend to be impetuous and impulsive. They often post things in the moment without giving much thought to the longer term. Many are unaware that these pictures and posts may remain on the Internet forever, even after they delete them from their social media pages. Someone else may have shared or copied it — and that photo of them behaving disgracefully at a party at the age of sixteen may not be suitable background information for a twenty-six-year-old in search of a new employer.

This is advice that we need to heed as parents as well: your child may be rightly apprehensive about launching himself into the job market with that picture of him on his potty still at large in cyberspace.

Ⓣime

Children spend so much time on social media every day. If they used that time to develop a skill, they would likely become an expert in a year or two. This is perhaps not a persuasive argument to use with teens, so it's probably more productive to get them to think about how social media time has to fit into the number of hours available in a day. They need a certain amount of time for school, sleep, eating meals, doing homework, etc., so spending such a large proportion of their waking hours online may mean that they are constantly chasing their tails — something for them to think about.

(Y)ourself

You need to ask yourself whether you're setting a positive example. If your children are competing with your screen for your attention, it will undermine all your arguments about the real world being more important than the virtual one. It will demonstrate that their claims on your time come a poor second.

Also, remember to respect the trust your child has placed in you if they've accepted your friend request on Facebook or allowed you to follow them online in some way: don't comment or contribute, unless approved by your child. Contributing is just not cool, and you will be unfriended in a heartbeat. It will be easier to monitor them if you're a silent witness and don't need to get someone else to stalk them on your behalf!

This question of respect also extends to consent for posting photos. If you are posting a photo with other people in it, including your child, make sure you obtain consent from them.

Keeping control

The following tips will help you stay on top of social media in your household. First, set an example.

 ❂ Set a timer for thirty minutes when you use social media. When the timer goes off, move on to doing something constructive. This way, you'll be practising what you preach.

⚙ Speak to your friends in the flesh or on the phone rather than online.

⚙ Leave your phone behind when you go out for a walk (if you need it, for safety perhaps, pop it on airplane mode or silent).

⚙ If necessary, use social media as a reward for completing mundane tasks you'd rather not be doing, for example the laundry or your tax return.

⚙ Plan what you are using social media for.

Doing these things will place you in a more authoritative position when it comes to regulating your teen's use of social media.

When it comes to your teen:

⚙ Limit the time they spend on it and don't let it interfere with their sleep.

⚙ Make sure they can keep 'cyber opinion' in perspective — vulnerable teens are all too susceptible to unkind criticism and advice from online sites.

⚙ Discourage use of devices at family mealtimes. These are your opportunity to relate to one another in the flesh in a relaxed atmosphere.

⚙ Do all you can to keep up with the latest apps, and to be aware of the ones your child is using. Some are safer than others, and those involving chat rooms may present risks. If your child knows you're concerned about their online safety and that you've also gone to the trouble of learning something that digital newcomers find challenging, they'll feel more confident approaching you for help. They'll be more likely to come to you if they have concerns or end up in a compromising situation.

SOCIAL MEDIA CHECKLIST

✿ Remember that safety is paramount: ensure younger children have online access only via a family computer and that appropriate filters are applied on all devices.

✿ Make sure your child understands that they shouldn't reveal personal details online.

✿ Get your child to think carefully about what they're posting, as they'll no longer have control of this content once it's shared.

✿ Explain to your child that virtual reality bears little relation to the real world.

✿ Limit the time you spend on social media, so as to be in a position to limit the time your child spends on social media.

Chapter 11

Dealing with Emotional Outbursts

Unexpressed emotions will never die. They are buried alive and will come forth later in uglier ways.

— *Sigmund Freud* —

I believe that how we interact with other people defines who we are. Being able to express our feelings without fear of reprisals helps us to maintain a healthy mindset. Our primitive brains have been programmed for both safety and comfort, and our five major 'negative' emotions — anger, sadness, fear, hurt, and guilt — are actually there for our benefit. All too often, when people express any of these emotions, we steer them away from them with comments such as, 'Oh, come on now, let's be positive,' or 'I don't think that's very helpful.' In effect, we're encouraged to stifle these feelings, and to not acknowledge them.

Take anger, for example. If we express it in the right way, it helps us release tension, both physically and emotionally. But anger can be mismanaged: it can be used as a tool, an instrument of power with which to threaten others. When our emotions, left unchecked, put our own and others' well-being at risk, it's time to address them by taking back control.

Wrongly handled, negative emotions can be terribly disruptive: they can ruin relationships, destroy trust and respect, damage reputations, prevent us from taking on new challenges, and hamper decision-making. When we feel too negative, our judgement is clouded. A surfeit of negative emotions can even make us ill.

This is as true for teens as it is for us. You are likely to benefit from the techniques in this chapter in your bid to steer the family calmly through the storms of adolescence. And sharing them with your teen will give them some tools to cope with the darker moods that are an inevitable part of growing up.

Sometimes we pressure our teens into sharing their emotions, yet when they do, or maybe if they share too much with us, we often react negatively. If they're disinclined to share their emotions with us, it may be because they're still responding to the sorts of injunctions they recall from their childhood: 'Stop crying,' 'Stop shouting,' or, worse still, 'You're just being naughty!'

You need to feel confident that dealing with your teen isn't going to provoke extreme reactions in yourself. It's best if you can model a positive approach to dealing with emotion. What follows is intended to help you reach the ideal balance between being responsive to emotion but not overwhelmed by it. From this position of strength you will be able to reach out to your teen.

Take back control

Although we can't control what happens to us, we can control how we respond to it (remember Event + Response = Outcome?). In doing so, we take back power. However, if we place the blame elsewhere and insist on remaining the victim, then we reject that power.

So how do we start that process? It's as easy as ABC.

(A)cknowledgement

Admitting that we have negative emotions is the first step to taking control of them. If you can recognise the signs, you can stop and take stock. The telltale physical symptoms might include a raised heart rate, shallow breathing, sweating, and even dizziness. Mental symptoms might include faulty reasoning and confusion. What these signs are telling you is 'Something is going on here and you need to do something about it.'

(B)elief

You need to believe that you can do something about it. As we've already established, our thoughts are liable to become our behaviour. If we are permanently on the negativity bandwagon, it will affect our behaviour. We have to believe that by changing our thoughts, we can also change our behaviour.

(C)atalyst

Identifying the catalyst for your emotional outbursts will help you to be prepared. Forewarned is forearmed, and if you can recognise the triggers, you can mitigate their effects. Is there a specific situation that makes you uneasy? Is there a particular person who drives you crazy? Are old feelings stirred up if you witness bullying or injustice? Do you feel especially vulnerable at certain times of the day? Sometimes it's not obvious to begin with; a lot of people find that keeping a journal helps. Writing things down enables you to identify the patterns in your thinking, to say, 'OK, this seems to trigger something: every time it happens I react in this way.'

The value of this process lies in that whatever the emotion, it works. People can have very different triggers and, perhaps more importantly, can respond to the same trigger in very different ways. One person's cause for sadness is another person's cue for anger.

LEARNING FROM THE ROMANS

The Romans gave us the useful saying *Mens sana in corpore sano*: a healthy mind in a healthy body. Our physical health and our mental health are closely intertwined, so regular exercise, a healthy diet, and enough sleep provide a good foundation for maintaining a balanced outlook on life. They better equip us to steer a steady course even when we find ourselves on an emotional roller coaster.

Once you've developed an understanding of how, when, and where you are vulnerable to emotional outbursts — fits of anger, panic attacks, or any other manifestation of excessive negative feelings — you can apply both a physical and a mental technique to regain control.

Make space

Give yourself some room to manoeuvre. You might be able physically to walk away from the situation, but if not, you need to switch off and mentally go to another place. This allows you to calm down and re-evaluate exactly what is happening.

Take a Breath

Concentrating on your breathing allows your mind to stop racing. Focusing mentally on rhythmical breathing interrupts the feelings of being overwhelmed, of panic, of helplessness, of fury — whatever it is that you're experiencing. It floods your body with serotonin, the hormone that makes us feel more relaxed. Just give this box-breathing exercise a try next time you're in a stressful situation.

Box breathing

Box breathing is a relaxation exercise that helps to calm the mind down when you're feeling really anxious or stressed. Here is what you do:

⚙ Imagine a box.

⚙ Trace the top of the box in your mind, and while you do …

⚙ … breathe IN slowly through your nose for a count of 4.

⚙ Trace down one side of the box in your mind and while you do …

- ⚙ … breathe OUT slowly through your mouth for a count of 4.

- ⚙ Trace the bottom of the box in your mind and while you do …

- ⚙ … breathe IN slowly through your nose for a count of 4.

- ⚙ Trace up the other side of the box in your mind and while you do …

- ⚙ … breathe OUT slowly through your mouth for a count of 4.

You can repeat this as many times as you need to.

Notice how your mind starts to calm down and you start to think clearly; notice how you are feeling less anxious.

■■■

These techniques disrupt your flow of negative thoughts. They form a useful strategy to deal with a whole host of situations. Whether you are paralysed with fear because a certain person has just walked into the room, or rigid with fury because some road hog has just cut you up, the principle is the same: bring on the pattern interrupt.

Repurposing emotions

Now that you're back on an even keel, use the three Is to fight back against overwhelming emotion.

(I)dentify

First, put a name to the emotion you're experiencing. Is it anger? Or is it guilt or resentment? (Both of these can be just as damaging as anger.) You need to put that emotion under the spotlight and interrogate it. Am I livid with so-and-so? Am I frustrated because once again I haven't got a promotion? Am I feeling guilty because I'm telling my child off? Once you've picked the emotion out from the identity parade, you can move on to the next phase.

(I)ntention

Negative emotions have a protective purpose, even if it might be a purpose at odds with modern life. The amygdala, the primitive area of the brain that generates emotions, is sending us an alert: 'Hey, the status quo isn't working here and we need to do something about it.' Only the situation it's warning us about, isn't as life-threatening as that sabre-toothed tiger or the theft of our winter rations by wild animals. Once you realise that your negative emotion has a positive purpose, you can look at it differently. You can start reframing the emotion and stop beating yourself up about it. You are no longer simply prey to an emotion, once you understand the warning you can act on it.

(I)ntensity

It is the intensity of the emotion as you experience it that gets you into trouble. Reducing this force will make the emotion manageable, and the techniques I've set out above will help to do this. Now you've begun to regain control, you can progress with reframing the emotions, and with cultivating an awareness of your triggers.

EMOTIONAL OUTBURSTS CHECKLIST

✿ Remember that negative emotions exist for our benefit; they just need to be handled right.

✿ Try not to react negatively when your teen expresses strong emotion.

✿ Analyse the emotion you're experiencing and why it's so intense to help you put it in perspective.

✿ Give yourself space and time to breathe deeply; this will help you deal with strong emotions.

✿ Model a calm approach when confronted with emotional outbursts to signal to your child that it's possible to take control of these emotions.

Chapter 12

Coping with Confusion

You can do anything — but not everything.

——————————————— *David Allen* ———————————

A couple of the definitions for confusion are 'uncertainty about what is happening' or 'a state of being bewildered or unclear in one's mind'. I often refer to this as 'overwhelm'. Perhaps you too can relate to this? It's not always a bad thing — we might be overwhelmed by lots of compliments or many offers of support. But the word usually has negative connotations. The challenge for us as parents is to be able to spot when our child is struggling, and, just as importantly, to know what we can do to help.

The ability to cope when you are overwhelmed is called resilience. It's vital to help your child to build up resilience, be it emotional or mental, so that they are better equipped to deal with difficulties, to bounce back from disappointments, and to learn from their mistakes. When overwhelmed, we are likely to feel frustrated or helpless, but how the adults cope sends an unmistakable message to our child. We, too, need to develop resilience in order to model for the child how best to manage the experiences of confusion and disorder. The following tips will help you guide your child when they too are struggling:

⚙ 'No man is an island'

Your child is not alone in having these feelings. One in five children experience some sort of emotional disorder, and it affects their life at school and within the family. Don't underestimate this: if a child is suffering, it has an impact on the whole family. But there is support out there for you and your family; there's no need to feel isolated.

⚙ Ask for help

Don't be scared to acknowledge that sometimes your child might need support from outside the family; all you have to do is ask. Although our egos may insist that we deal with an issue, we may not be the people best equipped for the task. Sometimes children find it hard to open up to their parents through fear of being judged negatively by them, or of disappointing them, or even of worrying them. (It's worth noting again that a significant number of young people I see as private clients require only one session; sometimes all they need is a bit of reassurance from someone who is an objective, unbiased observer.)

⚙ Don't blame yourself

Finally, remember that if your child is struggling with feeling overwhelmed, it doesn't mean you're a bad parent, or that your child is inadequate. Be kind to yourself and turn that negative energy around by directing it towards finding solutions. Remember that a happy and healthy parent serves the child better. If need be seek support for yourself too, whether it's a counsellor or a large glass of wine with friends.

Immediate action

So what's the first step?

Listen to your child and validate their feelings. Comforting a child can all too easily turn into trying to minimise their problems and sweep them under the carpet. Reassurances that 'Things will be fine' are not helpful. You probably wouldn't say this to a friend, so listen respectfully to what your child has to say, and engage with it fully.

Identify someone you trust. Make your child aware that however hard their pain gets, they are loved and supported. If you feel that they don't see you as the right person to offer this support — however much they might love you — find someone they can trust. If you have someone in mind, let your child know. My kids didn't want to tell me everything, but I knew that their uncle was a safe person for them to approach. I knew he would listen to them with love and without passing judgement. It was massively important for my kids to have someone like this, because sometimes I was the problem!

If a family member isn't an option, there are plenty of other trusted adults your child could go to, be it a family friend, your GP, or maybe an organisation such as YoungMinds or ChildLine. At school there are counsellors, people responsible for pastoral care, nurses, and teachers. Make sure your child understands they are not on their own, that there is a strong framework to support them.

Coping strategies

Before finding outside help in attempting to calm the mental chaos, there are simple, practical steps for you (and your child) can try. Think ABCDE:

(**A**)ctivities
(**B**)reathe
(**C**)hoose
(**D**)ialogue
(**E**)xercise

(**A**)ctivities

You need to be aware of what's making demands on your child's time and headspace. Kids often feel overwhelmed by all the expectations placed on them. They need to get the right grades so they've got to do homework; they might have extracurricular activities like music lessons, and/ or a place on the football team that they don't want to lose. On top of all that they need to nurture the right friendships, wear the right clothes, and go to the right places. If they have too much on their plate right now – sit with them and see what they can let go of – to alleviate these pressures.

Breathe

Your child needs to come up for air. There's a reason why breathing is a recurring theme throughout this book: stopping and focusing on the process of breathing itself creates space to take back control. And what's more, the well-oxygenated brain is far better equipped to think through options and make sound decisions.

Inhale / Exhale

Running through the following exercise with your child will do you both a power of good.

1. Put one hand on your chest and one hand on your tummy.

2. Take a deep breath, drawing the air right down into your abdomen so you can feel it expanding. Your lower hand will move outwards.

3. As you inhale and exhale, think of a random number — thirty-seven, say — and count slowly up to it.

4. If you need to feel calmer still, count back down from thirty-seven.

5. Continue to do this for as long as it takes to get you back on an even keel.

■■■

Choose

Give your child the tools to deal with the tasks in hand by prioritising. Ask them to choose one activity to do next — just one activity. For the time being they don't have to worry about getting their kit ready for football, or practising their scales, or whatever. Once they've completed that activity, they can choose another thing to do. They make the choice, and this gives them back focus and control. They are regulating the demands on them rather than letting the tide of demands wash over them.

(D)ialogue

Maintain the dialogue with your child, or if need be, establish it or re-establish it. Of course it's easier if you're in the habit of talking to them about their day. With small children, you can introduce the idea of butterflies and wasps. The butterflies are the good things ('I got a gold star today'; 'I saw next door's kitten in the garden'), and the wasps are the bad things ('I dropped my coat in a puddle'; 'Anna wouldn't sit next to me today'). This will get them into the habit of coming to you with the things that concern them, help them to acknowledge that things go wrong sometimes, and give them a sense of perspective. With older children you will obviously have to initiate conversations in a subtler way. Car journeys can be a good opportunity, as it's often easier for them to talk to you if they don't have to look you in the eye.

If your teen just cannot open up and talk to you, you could encourage them to start a dialogue with themselves by keeping a journal. Writing thoughts down can be therapeutic — a great way to resume order in a chaotic mind and environment. Whether they choose to write everything in a lovely journal or on a scrappy piece of paper that they later burn is up to them. It's the process itself that is cathartic.

(E)xercise

Exercise is vital because it releases all those feel-good hormones: the endorphins. If they're little, children might just need a good run around the park, or to play hide-and-seek up and down the house. Playing a sport is always a good thing, but for those who don't like team games, a walk in the woods or on the beach (a place where they can commune with nature) is good too. As well, there are fantastic yoga and exercise videos on YouTube that they can follow in the privacy of their own rooms. Once the endorphins start flowing, they restore balance in your head.

Have a plan

Children need to have a sense of control over their own lives, especially as they become older and need to explore their own independence. This control can reduce those feelings of uncertainty when things aren't going so well. By creating a plan they can introduce some order and predictability to their lives — in effect, a contingency plan. A younger child might use it when feeling a bit sad and worried about things; an older child might need it when having suicidal thoughts. A plan allows them to organise their thoughts and prepare for eventualities: 'When X happens, this is what I will do'; 'When I feel like this, I will …'

Happy list

A list of things that make your child smile — that make them feel happy and confident — gives them something they can immediately look at when the going gets tough. It could be a list of pictograms for a younger child to carry around in their schoolbag, or a written list for a teen to keep on their phone. This list will carry the message 'Life's not all bad'.

People list

A list of the people they can turn to for support — the people we discussed earlier in the chapter — is also useful for your child to have to hand. It should include telephone numbers and email addresses if appropriate. It should also specify the best person to turn to in any given situation: for example, if the issue is bullying, the form teacher is the first port of call; for an older child having suicidal thoughts or feeling anxious about drugs, the number of a relevant organisation or of a trusted adult is what's needed. This list means that, when their head's spinning, they don't have to spend ages hunting for information.

Some children might want to go to a safe space away from home, especially if there is unrest at home (e.g., due to a family member's drinking). If retreating to their room is not going to put enough distance between them and the source of their anxiety, the list will remind them that they can go to a neighbour's house, or perhaps to a friend's.

The printed word

Don't overlook printed material as a useful source of information and reassurance. It can be far more read-ily accessible than online material. Having leaflets from relevant organisations in the house means there is advice instantly to hand. And this material could provide good opportunities for discussion.

Printing out some of the exercises from this book is a good idea also — instant aide-memoires for box breathing, or the smile trick, discussed in Chapter 15, or whatever will help to steady your child. It's not easy to remember precise instructions if you're in a lather.

Task table

Finally, here's another practical exercise children can do to get back on top of everything. It's a little bit like a revision timetable, so the format itself may be familiar to them. Adults might also give it a go to see if it can bring some clarity to their time-poor existence!

⚙ **FIND** a piece of paper.

⚙ **WRITE** down all the tasks that you need to do and all the things that are overwhelming you in a column labelled 'Item'.

⚙ **CREATE** three more columns: Delete, Delegate and Due

⚙ **PAUSE** and take a break. Eat a sandwich, play with the dog, run around the block — this way, you pull out of the spiral of chaos rather than get sucked into it.

⚙ **EVALUATE** your tasks. Come back and look at each entry to decide what about it is so worrying. Some tasks you'll need to do, and we'll look at how you can deal with these in a minute. But some will be far more subjective: 'So-and-so was mean to me.' Something like that is in the past and you can't change it, so there's little point in worrying. (Calm reflection may reveal that this person is mean to everyone anyway!)

⚙ **CATEGORISE** your tasks. This is where your next three columns come in: 'Delete'; 'Delegate; and 'Due'. Move to the 'Delete' column all the things you can't change (and that you therefore shouldn't allow to drain your resources).

⚙ **ALLOCATE** each task to the appropriate category. Now you can decide which columns the tasks that must be completed belong in. Can someone else do any of these tasks? Move these to the 'Delegate' column (and ask those concerned to deal with it accordingly). Put the tasks that only you can do in your 'Due' column and prioritise. If that's still looking a bit scary, break these individual tasks down into bite-sized chunks. You have an 800-word assignment due next Tuesday? That's five days away, so why not write 160 words a day for the next five days? Not quite so scary.

⚙ **REMOVE** tasks from the first column once they've been dealt with. When everything in this first column is crossed off, you'll have a clear picture of how you're going to deal with what's left and the feeling of over-whelm should be well and truly in retreat.

TASK TABLE

ITEM	DELETE	DELEGATE	DUE
Write assignment			✓
Walk the dog		✓	
Speech went badly	✓		
Declutter wardrobes		✓	
Transfer funds		✓	
Organise debate			✓
Explain to Joe			✓
Phone Mary		✓	
History meeting		✓	
Contact Mrs Andrews			✓
Get keys cut		✓	
Reschedule paper	✓		

The longer view

Looking to the future can help your child maintain perspective about what is happening. It's worth reminding them how fulfilling life can be if you know who you are as an individual and what you want to achieve. Knowing these things will help them develop the confidence and resilience needed to place immediate threats or problems in a rational context: OK, they might have that nasty test on Thursday, but by Friday it will all be over and they'll have an exciting weekend ahead of them; their finals might be looming, but after that they'll never have to take another exam in their lives if they don't want to, and their time will be their own again.

Planning fun activities can help develop this outlook, as can encouraging them to find an activity they are passionate about. They will soon see progress that will reinforce a sense of purpose and a feeling that this skill is a constant that they can rely on despite what else is happening in their lives.

Visiting an elderly relative or family friend could take them temporarily out of their own world. Hearing about life experiences that are different from their own can be immensely enriching, especially if the person has experienced harsh and unpleasant things and survived. Perhaps there are even opportunities for your child to support that person in some way, which would enhance their sense of belonging and purpose.

CONFUSION CHECKLIST

⚙ Listen to your child if you suspect they're feeling overwhelmed; this is the first step.

⚙ Don't be afraid to seek outside help, whether from a professional or simply from a trusted adult your child would feel comfortable confiding in.

⚙ Teach your child coping strategies: breathing, planning out their tasks, prioritising.

⚙ Help them to discover a passion or an interest that will give them a sense of purpose and allow them to focus on the future.

⚙ Draw up contingency plans with them so that they need never feel out of control.

Chapter 13

How to Boost Body Image

I finally realised that being grateful to my body was key to giving more love to myself.

———————————————— *Oprah Winfrey* ——

The media loves to promote the notion of perfect — the perfect family, the perfect job, and not least, the perfect body shape. It puts us under pressure to match the ideals, but at what cost? In one sense, the prospect of the ideal raises the bar and makes us try harder, and there's no harm in that. As the saying has it, 'Shoot for the moon. Even if you miss, you'll land among the stars.' However, these aspirations have to be kept in perspective; otherwise, fear of failure can lead to paralysis.

Body image and self-esteem

Self-esteem is about how we value ourselves, whereas body image is about how we think others value us; it's about how we think we look. But it's low self-esteem that magnifies the tiniest of faults — bumps round the waistline, wayward hair, skin blemishes — into all-out catastrophes. It's no wonder that young people feel under pressure; they're surrounded by images of size-zero models on the catwalk and Olympians with six-packs (which have probably been Photoshopped beyond all recognition).

It's human nature to be more judgemental about our own physical attributes than others'. We need to stop battering our self-esteem by putting ourselves under the microscope. And we need our children to understand how the media influences them with the fake images it peddles. They should not feel burdened with a sense of inadequacy in failing to match the ideal.

It's hard to understand why our children would look in the mirror and not like what they see — we simply don't see what they do. Nevertheless, what they see is real for them. It might be natural to want to intervene, but we parents must recognise that we are in a no-win situation. If we offer advice, we risk sending our children the message 'You are broken, let me fix you'. On the other hand, the last thing we want to do is ignore them.

Love and acceptance are basic needs. It's our responsibility, as parents ensure that our children feel both loved and accepted for who they are as individuals. Because once they feel happy with being 'just themselves' the faster their self-esteem and confidence builds.

Weight problems

Children who feel under pressure to lose weight are highly susceptible to eating disorders such as bulimia and anorexia. Many resort to laxatives and appetite suppressants. What they may not understand is that their bodies haven't yet finished developing. Whether they're dieting, using steroids to bulk out, or exercising excessively to get just the right degree of muscle definition, they are in fact working on a moving target.

EATING-DISORDER CHECKLIST

Here are ten signs to look out for if you suspect your child is developing an eating problem:

- ✿ Are they reading food labels and focusing on healthy eating obsessively (orthorexia)?
- ✿ Do they lack focus and joy?
- ✿ Are they wearing baggy clothes that conceal their shape?
- ✿ Are they starting to look unhealthy?
- ✿ Are their sleep patterns more erratic?
- ✿ Are they becoming more withdrawn?
- ✿ Do they avoid eating out?
- ✿ Are they becoming critical of other people's eating habits?
- ✿ Are they exercising too frequently, trying to work off whatever they've eaten?
- ✿ Do they prefer to eat alone (or use the excuse that they've already eaten)?

This is a difficult and complex area, and parents need to be extremely subtle in their approach to tackling it. Studies show that parents are well-advised to not even broach the subject of weight or problems with body image. And I can endorse this with the voice of experience: well-meaning comments about my 'weight problem' when I was only about ten years old had a lasting impact. After several decades of running with the shame of this, my message is, don't go there. So what's the alternative?

Character building

A lot depends on what age group you're dealing with, but some approaches just can't be started too early. Even young kids often place too much emphasis on their body image and measure their value accordingly. It's up to us as parents to challenge these preconceptions, but covertly. The secret is to highlight your child's character and achievements, rather than their appearance. Focus on their personality with comments such as

- ✿ Oh, you are such a loyal friend.
- ✿ You're such fun to be with.
- ✿ You've worked so hard on that essay — well done!
- ✿ You're so good at cycling/baking/painting, etc.

All this builds up their confidence and their self-esteem, and helps to guard against their investing too much in their appearance.

Food

The diet industry is a multi-billion-pound business designed with failure in mind. Why does Weight Watchers have monthly subscriptions as well as annual ones? Because they know you'll fall off the wagon and they want you to keep coming back to them.

It's far better to help your child develop healthy eating habits right from the start, so that they never have to think about dieting. You can at least control what they eat at home. Watch what and how they eat. This couldn't be further from watching the numbers on the scales. Start a dialogue about healthy foods versus processed foods and the benefits of drinking water rather than fizzy drinks.

As parents it's our responsibility to provide healthy meals. Get rid of all the high-calorie snacks and fast foods, and think about providing the kind of home cooked meals your grandmother would have eaten and prepared. We should also consider more realistic portion sizes. Retailers are offering us larger portions for only a few pence more – this does not mean we have to eat it all in one sitting however! Children will be no less observant in this area than in any other, so I'm afraid you need to practise what you preach. You can't expect to your child to follow the rules if no one else in the family is prepared to.

Watch out for eating patterns you may have formed in your own childhood. Many of us were reared by parents who lived through war-time rationing and post-war austerity and therefore insisted that we eat everything on our plates.

Avoid using food as a reward. We are surrounded by examples of this: reward yourself for success in business with free food and booze in an airport lounge; reward yourself for the arduous task of doing your shopping with a free coffee. Within the home, we may use food as an emotional weapon. Many of us can relate to spending hours making a lasagne only for a child to turn their nose up at it. We respond with a wounded 'I made it especially for you.'

Mind your language

Even if you establish a healthy-eating routine and set an example by exercising, you may betray yourself through your language. Children have an unerring ability to pick up on mismatches between what we do and what we say, or to misinterpret what we've said in a predictably unhelpful way. You can undermine all your good work with an unguarded 'Does my bum look big in this?' type of question.

Children are mostly looking for reassurance rather than a critique, so accentuate the positive. The answer to their 'Does this make me look fat?' question should focus on how the outfit reflects their personality, or, at a pinch, how it matches the occasion it is designed for.

Be careful, too, of how you talk about people in the media, or people on the street. It doesn't take too many 'God, look at the state of her!' comments to undermine the non-judgement and acceptance message you are promoting at home.

However much you monitor your language, you may still be drowned out by the opinions of strangers: 'Oh, I wouldn't eat that because it's got way too many calories' or 'She'd be so much prettier if she lost some weight.' You need to say to your child, 'Do not listen to the opinions of strangers because they are just opinions. But if someone you love is concerned about your health or well-being then it is important to listen.'

Regaining control

Feelings of inadequacy (including problems with self-image) can lead children to self-harm (e.g., cutting or self-medicating.) It's their way of trying to get a sense of control over their own bodies. And in some cases, self-harm provides them with a real and immediate source of anguish to replace the far more insidious anguish in their heads.

We need to help them find a less destructive path out of victimhood. The following exercise should help them to break out of their spiral of self-loathing and self-pity.

Who do you think you are?

This exercise involves going a bit deeper. It's about digging underneath superficial, circular thinking that dwells on the negatives to uncover the buried positives. The format and content are fairly flexible; you can help your child come up with questions relevant to them. In this book we've discussed the need to reframe your thoughts. This exercise will help you do this systematically. After all, where have your child's negative thoughts got them so far?

WHO DO YOU THINK YOU ARE?

BODY:
* Legs - helped me come second in the cross-country
* Hair - YAY! Curls are in!
* Waist - core strength helps me in the gym

PEOPLE:
* Julie - we love going to the movies together
* Sister Sophie - she loves it when I read her a story
* Granny - she's always calm, whatever I do or say

HOPES/DREAMS:
* To enter a singing competition in the next year
* To study engineering at university
* To go to Canada

ACHIEVEMENTS:
* Made delicious pancakes on Pancake Day
* Learned to skate
* Got an A for my project in Physics

●●●

By the time they have completed this exercise, your child should have a far clearer sense of themselves as a unique and valuable person in the world. It should give them a sense of purpose, and of goals they can be working towards. Perhaps complete it in a journal so it's always accessible as a boost and a reminder.

Make sure your child understands that the unique, rounded individual that emerges from this exercise is the person that you and others will always love and value. Help them understand that there is a future for them out there for the taking.

BODY IMAGE CHECKLIST

✿ Be aware of eating-disorder symptoms.

✿ Promote healthy eating at home — and practice what you preach.

✿ Mind your language: compliment your child on accomplishments and character rather than appearance.

✿ Get your child to reframe the way they see themselves by getting them to value their body, their relationships, their achievements and their hopes and dreams.

✿ Reinforce the message that your child is unique and will always have your love.

Chapter 14

Peer Pressure and Socialisation

The quality of your life is a direct reflection of the expectations of your peer group.

———————————————— *Tony Robbins* ———

As children grow, their friendships can develop at an alarming rate. Kids are like sponges; they soak up influences from a range of sources, not all of which we may be happy with.

Friends

From birth to about seven years old, a child is exposed mainly to those in their home, so they adopt the parents' and carers values and beliefs. When they go to school, they are exposed to a far wider environment. From the ages of seven to fourteen, they will get input from friends, naturally, but also from teachers, youth leaders, and perhaps those in year groups above theirs. From the age of fourteen until they leave school, children rely a great deal on their friendships. They become hugely susceptible to pressures from their immediate peer group. Although the experience of girls is slightly different from that of boys as they embark on their teenage journey, friendships are everything for this age group.

At school, teens form a social foundation that will see them through their transition to independence. They look to their peers for help, and to reaffirm who they are as individuals. They place huge importance on fitting in and on having a sense of belonging within their group. They will tend to mimic their friends' behaviour: their mannerisms, the clothes they wear, the music they listen to, and the language they use.

Problems arise if your values and beliefs are not in line with those of your child's changing environments. The question is, how on earth, as parents, do we deal with that? First of all, we need to understand that from a biological perspective, our children are programmed to start pulling away from us. To prepare to stand on their own two feet, they need to start breaking their emotional ties with their parents. Although this can be alarming and painful, it's perfectly normal. In fact, it's our role to facilitate this process, and to make it as smooth as possible for our child.

Bear in mind that while our kids are trying to work out who they are, and while their brains are still developing, they will probably make some rather questionable decisions — choosing their friends will be no exception. Remember that up to a point, you need to allow your child to make their own mistakes so that they can learn from them and be better equipped to face the future.

To avoid feeling isolated, your child will naturally gravitate towards certain friendship groups. You may even hear them labelling cliques within their year group at school: the sporty ones, the musical ones, the nerdy ones, the popular ones, and so on. This again, is totally normal. If you look at your own friendship groups, you may recognise the pattern: perhaps you've got the Pilates gang, or the mother and toddler group, or the biking buddies. We like to be with like-minded people. We are tribal beings, and your child is no different. There is nothing worse than feeling that you don't fit in — and any group might be better than none.

Choices and accountability

Remember that not all peer pressure is necessarily negative. Your child might be influenced by friends who are working hard and aiming for good grades. The trick is to guide your child to make the right choices without making them feel that you're breathing down their neck.

Children observe their peers as much as they observe their family, so it's not surprising that they learn from them. The pressure of 'everyone else is doing it' may be enough to influence your child. Their reasons for giving in to peer pressure, regardless of whether it's against their better judgement, are no different from ours as adults: we want to be liked, we want to fit in, we want to keep the peace.

It's also not surprising that they will want to try new things at a time when they're trying to cut the apron strings.

So what do you do if you feel your child is being influenced by a bad crowd? Try to get to know that crowd a bit better, for a start. When I was a teenager, my parents made our home as welcoming as possible for my friends. This was reassuring for me. As I often felt out of my depth and unsure where I fitted in (and therefore very susceptible to peer pressure), I loved hanging out with friends in my safe place.

It's important for your child to learn, and accept, that they are accountable for their own behaviour. Even if you know that their friends are pulling the strings, that doesn't let your child off the hook. This is an important precedent to set. It reinforces the notion that actions have consequences, and that includes their choice of friends. The response to the constant lament 'So-and-so is allowed to do … ' is that you are not so-and-so's parent, and you remain in charge while they are still children.

Being in charge may just entail setting stricter boundaries if you find your child is getting out of their depth. Perhaps it's time to set some rules about when and where they can see their friends. The earlier you have these difficult conversations the easier future conversations may become, because from an early age they have an understanding of what you regard to be acceptable behaviour and what is not. You also need to make arrangements to keep your child safe when you aren't around, particularly a younger child. Make sure they have the phone numbers of people who can help (see Chapter 12, on feeling overwhelmed). Finally, remember that most teenagers aren't going completely off the rails and getting into trouble; at a time when they want to feel like adults, kicking off about curfews and other restrictions is understandable.

Boundaries

We need to set boundaries to establish a degree of order in the household. We need to clarify what is acceptable and what is beyond the pale. But make sure the boundaries are about health and well-being, not petty rules.

Timing is everything. Teenagers will resist bitterly a curfew imposed with a day's notice for a long-awaited party, so it's far better to discuss it with them well in advance. As mentioned above, the earlier you have these conversations the better.

Make sure your child understands the consequences of breaking the rules, and establish your course of action if the rules are broken.

What do you do if your rules are disobeyed? Above all, don't negotiate. If your teen spots a chink in your armour, they will chip away at it with all the tenacity of a Rottweiler. If they think you might back down, they will never give up. I know many children accuse their parents of being unfair, too strict, and of embarrassing them as a result, but deep down they appreciate that there are rules. Rules let them know where they stand, and above all, that you care.

Teach them to say no

This might be a lot easier than you imagine! As a teenager, I managed to miss a lot of parties and gatherings that I didn't want to go to just by saying, 'Oh, my mum's such a cow; she won't let me go.' Sometimes kids just need an excuse to say no, so if you can lend them your spoilsport ogre persona for this purpose, you might be doing them a favour!

If they want to say no to something a bit more complex (e.g., drugs), it might be a good idea to help them practice. Role play will help them negotiate these trickier conversations that they might be reluctant to have with their friends.

It can be tough to be the one who says no because it might mean standing out from the crowd. Some children can handle feeling isolated, but others can't. Encourage your child to team up with a buddy who has the same values. There is safety in numbers, and it might be easier for them to say no with someone else.

Giving your child a way out (X-Plan)

This is a fantastic exercise, that is attributed to Bert Fulks, Father, Teacher and Educator (www.bertfulks.com). It is a wonderful remedy for situations where your child might find things starting to get out of hand and they don't know how to get out of it without looking stupid.

This situation was familiar to my 15-year-old self, whether it was playing hooky from school or social situations. I still remember my first time at a beach party with older kids.

I was way out of my depth – but didn't want to lose face. It seemed easier to swig the Martini Bianco, rather than leave on my own with my tail between my legs and turn into that social pariah I dreaded becoming.

For this very reason this tool is a lifeline for many awkward teenagers. Here's how it works:

✿ Have two or three designated adults and put their mobile numbers in your child's phone. (Mum, Dad, older sister – whatever works)

* If anything makes your child uncomfortable about the situation they are in, they are to send the letter 'X' in a text message to *any* of these numbers.

* Whoever receives this text has to follow this basic script :

In a couple of minutes phone the child's mobile. When he answers the conversation goes like this:

"Hello?"

"Hey, –something's come up and I have to get to you right away."

"What's happened?"

"I'll tell you when I get there. Be ready to leave in five minutes. I'm on my way."

*Now your child tells his friends that he has to go – and is able to blame that 'spoilsport ogre persona'.

The bottom line is that your child knows that they have a way out, offering them the sense of security and confidence to navigate adolescence – whilst you still have their back – from a distance.

⚙ The next part is golden: You child can tell you as much – or as little – of that situation as they like. This plan only holds water if it comes with the agreement that there is no judgement and no reprisals. The caveat is if someone's life is in danger then they have to come clean – but otherwise they do not have to expand. Ever.

■■■

Believe me when I say this builds trust which in turn leads to more openness and transparency. If a child is in fear of punishment or judgement they are less likely to seek help – which may lead to graver consequences than the initial offence of being somewhere they shouldn't be, for example.

Values

Part of treading your way through the adolescent minefield is giving your teen space to tap into their own feelings and recognise what they believe to be right and wrong. Hopefully the open dialogue you establish will give them the critical thinking skills to analyse issues and make up their own minds. Just make sure they know that you're there for them. Let them know you're more inclined to trust their judgement than not so that they can make the right call without too much pressure from interfering parents.

Above all, applaud your child's choices when they are brave enough to follow their beliefs rather than the crowd.

Fitting in

Parents often say to me, 'My child isn't going out at the weekends. Does that mean that he's a social outcast?' There is absolutely nothing wrong with this. You could ask yourself the same question. If you come home after a long, stressful day, would you rather head out with your mates or settle down on your own, or with your family, at home? The answer to this question depends entirely on whether you're an introvert or an extrovert — and therefore, on how you recharge your batteries.

* **Extroverts** recharge their batteries around other people. At the end of a long day, they love nothing better than to let their hair down, surround them- selves with others, and feed on their energy.

* **Introverts** may be fine in social situations some of the time, but at the end of an intellectually, socially, or physically taxing day, they may need to be on their own to recharge.

Introverts are under siege in a society that expects instant displays of emotion and effusiveness. Through sites such as Facebook, there is an increased expectation of having lots of friends — and, by extension, lots of invitations. Your home should provide a safe space for a teen who at times prefers to retreat rather than go out and be gregarious.

It's up to you as a parent to distinguish between entirely normal introvert behaviour and any added pressure your child might be under. It doesn't hurt to bring their friends into your orbit, so that these teens can get some inkling of your family values. A good way of doing this is hosting

163

a party. I did this with our son, making it absolutely clear that although I wouldn't be present at the party, I would still be on the premises (and I was able to rely on our daughter to bring me dispatches from the front). It shows your child that you trust them, and that you are willing to meet them halfway.

PEER PRESSURE CHECKLIST

✿ Accept that as your child enters their teens, their friendship groups will exert an increasing amount of pressure on them.

✿ Get to know your child's friends and what makes them tick.

✿ Allow your child to make their own mistakes, but be there for them as a safety net.

✿ Make sure your child understands that they have the capacity to choose but that choices come with consequences.

✿ Set clear boundaries that your child can see the need for.

✿ Teach your child to say no; if need be, role play to prepare them.

✿ Have an exit plan agreed to give your child a sense of control.

Chapter 15

How to Manage Stress

It is not stress that kills us — it is our reaction to it.

— Hans Selye —

Millennials have the world in the palm of their hand. They have immediate access to people and information worldwide. They can find answers to the problems their homework throws up. They can research eating disorders and self-harm. They can get support from friendship groups in various forums. All this is on tap, night and day.

So why are our children so stressed – and why are they suffering from anxiety and depression in increasing numbers?

The academic pressures are unrelenting: children face endless tests and exams. They have no time to relax, to take their foot off the pedal. Our kids are physically and emotionally stressed, and according to the Samaritans, suicide is the second commonest cause of death amongst 15-19-year-olds worldwide. School counselling services are stretched to the limit and, more often than not, have huge waiting lists.

Millions of students sit exams each summer but recent reports from ChildLine suggest concerning statistics about how young people are trying to cope with the upcoming pressures that accompany exam season.

Further research indicates that it's not just exams and school pressures that affect our youngsters. Findings from the University of Manchester's National Confidential Inquiry into Suicide and Homicide by People with Mental Illness (the first time experts have studied the contributory factors on this scale) show there are an array of issues affecting the mental wellbeing of our children, including:

✿ physical health conditions such as acne or asthma

✿ bereavement

✿ bullying, mostly face to face.

The same study also found that 23% had used the internet in relation to suicide – including searching for methods or posting suicidal thoughts.

At least the prevalence of these problems has been acknowledged. And today there is far greater awareness and acceptance of mental health as a serious issue, for both children and adults. This new openness has made it far easier for individuals to seek solutions and ask for help. The Aviva Health of the Nation Index (2013) shows that 84% of GP appointments are related either directly or indirectly to stress and anxiety.

What is stress?

Like negative emotions, stress isn't all bad. It's the body's early warning system and it shouldn't be ignored. It's an unmistakable sign that things need to change. Stress can manifest itself as

- ✿ emotional stress, with symptoms such as anxiety, panic attacks, and depression;

- ✿ physical stress, with symptoms such as nausea, insomnia, and high blood pressure; and

- ✿ mental stress, with symptoms such as loss of confidence, mood swings, and poor concentration.

The causes of stress are wide-ranging, and different for everyone. One person's fast-paced, chaotic workplace can be another's highly stimulating and congenial environment. Some people are undone by a lack of sleep, whereas Margaret Thatcher famously thrived on only four hours a night. Some people are happy with their own company, while others feel a sense of panicky isolation if left on their own.

So, how can we minimise stress? Personally, I don't condone eliminating it altogether. I believe, we should aim to have a healthy balance, where it serves its protective function, keeping us alert and performing at our best while not overwhelming us. Self-care is the key to standing up to stress.

Self-care

What follows is useful for you, a responsible adult setting the pattern for your family. And it is useful for your teen, who must be equipped to withstand the rigours of modern adolescence. Effective self-care is based on the five S's: sleep, stretch, support, sustenance, and serenity.

(S)leep

Sleep helps our body to repair itself and our mind to process our experiences. Without sleep, our thinking is woolly and our judgement clouded. Remember that teens are likely to need a lot more sleep than you think; an early start for school should mean an early night. Not looking at electronic devices for an hour before going to bed helps the mind relax — possibly an unpalatable truth for a teen! Cut them a bit of slack at the weekends, too, as they're bound to have some catching up to do.

(S)upport

If you or your teenager is struggling, get some support, be it from the school, another trusted adult, your GP — whoever is appropriate. By keeping quiet, people often won't want to intrude or get involved. But if you reach out, you'd be surprised at how many people are there to support you: professionals, such as your doctor or the school counselling service, or trusted lay people, such as a fellow parent or a best friend.

(S)tretch

Exercising regularly releases the feel-good hormone serotonin and reduces levels of the stress hormone cortisol in the body. People who go to their doctor with depression are often advised to get out into nature for a twenty-minute walk each day, which helps stimulate the release of serotonin.

(S)ustenance

Like it or not, a healthy diet is vital for combating stress, as is being well hydrated. I'm sure I don't need to tell you which are healthy foods and which are junk. As to eating patterns, these are personal. Stick with whatever works best for you — and recognise that it will not necessarily be the same for your children. Some people thrive on eating little and often, while others swear by three meals a day with no snacks in between. Everyone's metabolism is different; just make sure you and your children are refuelling on a regular basis with good food and water.

(S)erenity

You need to maintain calm in your head to give yourself the space and peace to think straight. Constant interaction with electronic devices keeps the mind on high alert. Dropping everything, even just for five to ten minutes during the day, to meditate or stare aimlessly into the middle distance can be very restorative.

The smile trick

It's hard to have a negative thought when you're smiling.

This exercise harnesses the power of the unconscious mind; it helps you 'fake it till you make it'.

Place a pen horizontally in your mouth and hold it there for at least a minute through gritted teeth — with your lips apart! Your unconscious mind will be tricked into thinking that you're actually smiling and that therefore, all is well. It will send the signal to release more serotonin into the body, helping you to relax.

Notice how you very quickly feel more relaxed and calmer.

Give it a whirl — it only takes a minute.

•••

Anxiety and your child

Even though it's assumed that young people aren't subject to the stressors that bedevil adult life, the figures tell a different story. One in eight children suffers from anxiety, and it rises to one in four for teens. Anxiety is more prevalent among girls, and, tellingly, more prevalent among children with anxious parents. Anxiety is a learned behaviour; children learn how to use anxiety to get themselves out of a tight spot.

How can we tell if our child is suffering from anxiety? Look out for warning signals such as interrupted sleep, unexplained ailments on schooldays, stomach pains, and headaches. Watch out for patterns — maybe these symptoms appear on Wednesdays, when they don't want to take part in a certain activity. It's a matter of understanding what makes them anxious and why. Obsessive behaviour (e.g., clicking lights on and off, compulsive hand-washing, or perfectionism), should also ring alarm bells.

Minor changes may be enough to tip a child into anxiety. These changes may seem insignificant to us, but if we view them in the same light as a house move or a change of job, we'll get a better appreciation of their scale in the eyes of our child.

If you're an anxious parent, consider what makes you anxious; chances are, the same things will be making your child anxious. Children who have a fear of spiders may simply be emulating the fear of a parent who can't stand them.

Anxiety should be managed rather than eliminated because it keeps us alert. But if it becomes too strong, it stops us from doing things — that's when we have a problem and risk full-blown stress and panic attacks.

See off a panic attack

A panic attack is a sudden feeling of overwhelming anxiety. It can be debilitating, and can stop you in your tracks. Panic attacks are disconcerting for those experiencing them because they can happen rapidly and without warning.

The science behind them comes back again to the protective mind. If your mind thinks that your safety or comfort is compromised it goes into overdrive, and this can trigger a panic attack. Our adrenal gland will start pumping adrenaline and cortisol through the body in preparation for fight or flight. The recognisable signs are increased heart rate, shallow or laboured breathing, nausea, confusion, and sweaty palms. This whole process lasts about three minutes, until the body can't pump any more of these substances round. So how do we cope with all that?

Four steps to handling a panic attack

If a panic attack is imminent, this process will stop it in its tracks and keep it from escalating.

Step one: relax

It's easier said than done, but concentrate on your breathing. Aim for slow, deliberate breaths. This calms your mind.

Step two: stop

Mentally shout 'Stop!' — if you don't mind who hears you, you could shout it out loud. This interrupts the panic and gives your mind something to think about other than, 'I've got to get out of here. I'm going to be sick!'

Step three: talk positively to yourself

You need to reframe that negative feeling. Instead of thinking 'Help! Get me out of here — I can't cope,' say to yourself, 'Hang on a minute. This has happened to me before and I'm going to be OK.' You could rationalise the situation to yourself: 'I've never been sick yet, so I'm not going to be sick now.'

Step four: wait

If you can focus on the knowledge that these feelings will subside in three minutes, you can ride out the attack without prolonging it. The last thing you want to do is fuel it and keep the cycle going. Notice when the symptoms start subsiding, so that you know you will soon be back in control.

■■■

I think it's fair to say that children and teens are under far more pressure than they were a generation ago. Let them see that you understand this, and that you are on their side. Share with them the techniques that help you as an adult to cope with stress (it's also likely that adults are under far more pressure than they used to be) and support them every inch of the way. This way, you will sustain both their confidence and the positive relationship between you.

STRESS CHECKLIST

✿ Remember that stress is an early warning system telling you to make changes.

✿ Look out for the tell-tale signs of stress in your child: disrupted sleep, unexplained aches and pains, and withdrawal.

✿ Deal with stress, your own or your teen's, through self-care — enough sleep, healthy food, and exercise.

✿ Regain control through mental calm when stress is threatening you.

✿ To ward off a panic attack, start with focused breathing.

Chapter 16

Minimising Conflict

Not everything you fight about is worth fighting for.

————————————— *Aaron Anderson* ————

Conflict arises from a lack of communication. Very few of us have been taught to communicate effectively, so it's to be expected that we will come across some difficulties. So far we've addressed listening (see the exercise on reflecting, in Chapter 7), and helping your child to make their own decisions. (see the exercise, Critical Thinking Mode in Chapter 9). But there's likely still unfinished business when it comes to improving communication within the family. The next step is being able to head off conflict.

A word of warning, though: when it comes to conflict, your teenager will probably be great at playing the victim. Children who do not get their own way are good at pulling on the heartstrings: 'Everyone else is doing this! Why do you have to make me so unpopular?' or 'Oh please, this is so unfair!' Just remember that the more you fan the flames of conflict, the brighter they will burn. The trick is to defuse the situation as soon as possible.

Remember also that children are experts at playing one adult off against another. If Mum says they can't go out, they'll ask Dad, who may just say yes. The secret here is not to do battle with your partner in front of the children. Accept that on this occasion you've been defeated and establish a system to prevent this from happening again.

Conflict in the family can emerge in a number of ways. Make sure, if you can, that it's not arising between the adults. Children learn by observation, and if they're constantly seeing arguing adults, they will grow up believing this is normal behaviour. If the arguments are occasional, that's absolutely fine — and even quite useful. It's healthy for kids to see that friction can be resolved and life can proceed amicably afterwards.

The golden rule is that if one parent is already dealing with a problem, make sure the other one doesn't get involved – unless circumstances demand that both adults need to show a united front, perhaps to fulfil a supporting role. If there are conflicting opinions between adults, ensure that these issues are addressed away from the child – as previously stated – your teenager has the determination of a small terrier if they spot a weakness in the 'opposition'.

Inevitably, divorce and separation make all this a lot more complicated. In this situation, it's perfectly OK however, to have a 'different parent, different rule' regime. Things aren't always cut and dried (this is a great life lesson), but make sure that everyone is clear about the distinction between the two sets of rules before your child can exploit them and catch you out.

Looking behind the behaviour

One way of finding a path through conflicts is to understand that behind the negative behaviour there is a positive intention. Sometimes it may be easily identifiable (if not altogether welcome). At other times the positive intention might not be so obvious: the antagonism that they are displaying towards you might spring from a different motivation than the one you imagine. Much conflict with your child may stem from the fact that they are simply trying to prolong an interaction with you.

This is especially true of girls, who tend to strike up more arguments than boys and maintain contact through the ping-pong-ball exchanges of a flaming row. For them, even bad attention is better than no attention at all. Boys, tend to prefer less drama and may often need to withdraw from an argument, hence the door-slamming and disappearing into their room. There's no escaping the fact that all this goes with the territory of adolescence.

Minimising conflict

There's no hope of eradicating conflict when you have adults in the making growing up in the house. Minimising it is a more realistic goal.

To set the foundation for minimising conflict, establish clear ground rules — whether it's for curfews, helping round the house, whatever — and sound reasons for those rules. They are not negotiable; any negotiation is likely to become a fight. It's a matter of managing your child's expectations;

conflict is most likely to arise when their expectations are not being met. By setting the ground rules early, you minimise last-minute surprises and subsequent slanging matches.

If our children want to be treated like adults, we parents need to start getting them to think like adults. Agreeing to rules with them is like drawing up a contract. If you've sat down with them and worked through the rules, maybe tweaked them in response to any good points they've made, you're far more likely to get buy-in from them.

In my experience, punishments rarely have a positive effect. They just seem like parents' last-ditch attempts to assert their authority, and end up breeding resentment.

What we want to do is teach our children to manage their behaviour. When a child receives a punishment they are more likely to focus on their anger with you rather than how they behave in the future.

Consequences help the child to make a better decision next time – letting them take responsibility for their own actions. Consequences give your child the opportunity to learn from the lesson rather than just harbour negative emotions.

To the parent who says, 'But they're always pushing my buttons!' I would respond, 'Event + Response = Outcome.' Perhaps by changing your own mindset and behaviour, you all could benefit from these adjustments. Alongside firm rules, you need a degree of flexibility in applying them to allow for countless variables — your children getting older, for a start.

Also, know when to pick your battles. You don't have to

win every time, and you may need to ask yourself if you're bringing your own baggage to the table. The easiest way to resolve conflict is to remove emotion and ego. If you're feeling disregarded and belittled, that's your problem, and nothing to do with your teenager. It's worth acknowledging that.

The seven golden rules

1. Be calm
Children rarely listen when they're being yelled at, and at this stage they're far too grown-up for that — they'll probably just shut down. (Remember also that being shouted at can be very frightening for younger children.)

2. Focus on the outcome
Work out what you want your child to understand about the rules. You set a curfew for their safety, not because you want to curb their social life. You insist that they study and do homework so that they'll have positive choices ahead of them when they finish school, not because you are trying to railroad them and spoil their fun.

3. Acknowledge their feelings
If your child is kicking off, it's likely because they're feeling insecure. You need to connect with them emotionally, and perhaps even physically, to show them that you're on their side. They'll receive messages that their behaviour is out of order far better if they're confident that you love and value them.

4. Avoid physical punishment

This is a no-brainer. Smacking doesn't work and is just not acceptable. When you lose control it's game over, and they will have won. Also, children and young people are now far more aware of their rights. They know that this is unacceptable behaviour on your part.

5. Do not isolate your children

Tempting though it is to tell children to go to their room, or to get out of your sight, don't give into it. As previously mentioned some children feel the only way they can grab your attention is by behaving badly. By isolating them, you are just fanning their insecurities. Far better to keep them in the room with you and say, 'One minute of time out. I won't say anything, and you won't say anything, and in the meantime, let's practise the box breathing.'

6. Take an objective view

Take the heat out of the situation with your child by looking at it first from their point of view, then from your point of view, and finally from a third-party point of view, removing all ego and emotion from it. Encourage your child to do the same. This may well reveal that you are making a mountain out a molehill, the flaw in the argument of one side or another, or the real source of the problem.

7. Lead by example

Try not to get stroppy and hot-headed. If you do, make sure you apologise. It sends a powerful message: you do not claim to be infallible, you have the humility to acknowledge this, and you make reparation when you've done something wrong.

Sibling rivalry

You will have heard the old adage 'You can choose your friends, but you can't choose your family'. Well, that is especially true of siblings, who can sometimes feel like they've just been thrown together with the expectation that they will get on. Sibling rivalry often arises when one child feels their relationship with their parent is being compromised by their brother or sister.

You probably won't be able to prevent all conflict between siblings, as this is how kids test the water in life. Home and family is the very first environment in which your child can flex their muscles and start learning about 'survival of the fittest' It's how they build inner resilience. Kids bicker, kids argue, kids fight — wherever possible leave them to it. They will usually work it out, and if you intervene, you may be accused of taking sides. Intervene only if you think someone is in danger.

But you still need to recognise the disparities between your children and be sensitive to them. Sources of conflict can include the following:

- ✿ Position in the family: the oldest one may feel burdened with responsibility, whereas middle children can be relatively carefree and the baby of the family can get away with murder.

- ✿ Gender: are you falling into the trap of treating your children according to outdated stereotypes? Perhaps you're more sensitive towards your daughter but encourage your son to take a more rough-and-tumble approach to life?

181

✿ Age: is an older child feeling held back by the concessions that must be made for younger ones?

These are just three examples of issues that could be upsetting the equilibrium and generating discord in the family.

Fairness

Many parents feel that fairness and equality reduce conflict. This is not necessarily true; there is a difference between being fair and treating children equally. Throughout this book I've stressed the need to honour and respect your children's individuality, and this is just as necessary in the area of sibling rivalry. The checklist below will ensure that you are treating each child according to their needs.

THE EVEN-HANDED PARENT

✿ Don't have favourites: assess your children as individuals and tailor your treatment of them accordingly.

✿ Set the ground rules for acceptable behaviour between siblings, and involve your children in the process.

✿ Let them know that life isn't always fair, and that there will be times when one sibling needs more support than the others.

✿ Be there for each child and acknowledge that their needs are different.

✿ Celebrate their differences.

✿ Recognise that children need space, and may often need to be apart from one another.

✿ Avoid comparisons between your children.

✿ Give each child one-to-one attention, which will reduce the need for them to compete.

✿ Listen to each side of an argument.

If sibling conflict is really disrupting your family life, it might be worth seeking professional help. Bullying within families is rare, but it's wise to keep an eye out for the child who is throwing their weight around too much and intimidating a sibling or siblings. The following are signs to watch out for:

- ✿ One child always avoids another.
- ✿ The conflict is always between the same children.
- ✿ There are changes in your child's appetite, behaviour, sleep patterns, etc.
- ✿ One child is particularly withdrawn.

Family meetings

A great way to keep on top of sibling conflict and ensure that it doesn't undermine the family is to hold a weekly family meeting.

It's a way of resolving conflicts that have arisen through-out the week, and it allows the family to work together to make decisions. The ground rules for the meeting should be agreed to at the start:

- ✿ no name calling;
- ✿ everyone's feelings have value;
- ✿ everyone has a voice;
- ✿ no one has to talk; and
- ✿ everyone has to listen.

■■■

Some degree of conflict is part of family life with teenagers, and sometimes it's beyond your control, but how it affects your family and the relationships within it is totally up to you. The most important thing is to remain flexible and open to dialogue with your child. What is your ultimate goal here? It's a happy, well-balanced young adult with whom you want to have a functioning and healthy relationship once they've navigated this minefield of adolescence.

CONFLICT CHECKLIST

⚙ Head off conflict as early as possible; listening and communicating are the best ways to do this.

⚙ When conflict with your partner arises, show your children that some friction is inevitable but that reconciliation is always around the corner. Do not let it escalate, though.

⚙ Try to understand what lies behind the conflict.

⚙ Do not lose your temper or strike your child: both are counterproductive.

⚙ Treat your children fairly and don't let sibling rivalry get out of hand.

Chapter 17

Sex, Drugs and Drink

Alcohol: temporary fun with permanent consequences.

In the teenage years, the prefrontal cortex is still developing; this part of the brain helps them make decisions and solve problems and does not mature until the early twenties for girls and mid-twenties for boys. In the meantime, the amygdala, which responds instinctively, is working overtime. As a result, our teenagers, in their bid for independence, are likely to take risks and make some foolish decisions, not least about sex, drugs, drink, and smoking.

Sex, hormones and puberty

Puberty is nature's way of preparing our children for independence. They change physically: they get taller, more muscular, and hairier — we've all been there. They change emotionally, too: they become more unpredictable, louder or quieter, and their interest in their sexuality changes. This can be a scary time for parents, but we need to guide them through the haze of hormones.

> According to the Office for National Statistics (2017), the UK has the highest teen birth rates in Europe.

Girls' and boys' minds are wired differently when it comes to sex with boys generally being more focused on the physical act and less on the context and relationship. However, don't blame or shame boys about sex as it's a natural part of their development. This interest may well show itself at an earlier age than you expect;. because we live in a digital age it's likely that online porn will be their introduction to sex. This is why it's important to talk to your kids about sex when they're young.

Let's face it, it's never too early to talk to your child about the birds and the bees. The information you give them should be age-appropriate, but the sooner you broach the subject, the less taboo it will be. Gone are the days when you could afford to be prudish and not talk to them about S-E-X. If you don't discuss these issues with them, someone else will and the message you may want your child to hear may become distorted.

Many pre-teens or younger teenagers are convinced that they know it all anyway. They will talk about sex at school, and may have got their wires crossed. It's up to you to set them straight, and to take them through the physical and emotional changes they are likely to experience so that there are no surprises.

Children may know the nuts and bolts of sex, but what they can't know is how they will feel about it, so this is an important area to cover. Of course, sex can be fun and exciting, but they also need to find out about romantic love, and the relationship between sexual feelings and emotional attachment.

Safe sex

Many teenagers don't consider that having sex is necessarily a big issue. If they want to have sex, they will, even if they have to be sneaky about it. Many of their experiments in sex might be little more than a bid to push the boundaries just to see what happens. It's hard for a parent to hear this, but if your child is going to have sex you need to accept the fact and make sure they can do so safely. This entails educating them about the risks. And if you feel that they're somewhat apprehensive about dipping their toe in the water, reassure them that not all teenagers are sexually active! Making space for in-depth discussions of the following topics will be immensely valuable:

✿ their sexuality

✿ their attitude towards sex

✿ the legal age of consent

✿ unwanted pregnancy and contraception

✿ AIDS and other sexually transmitted diseases

✿ emotional complications

✿ mutual consent

This last point is vital. Children need to understand that their feelings and opinions matter, and that no one should be allowed to coerce them into doing anything they are not happy with. Explain to them that they have control, and that it is important to respect their bodies and feelings — no really does mean no. These discussions will equip them to stand their ground when the time comes, and could spare them a lot of grief.

From a purely practical perspective, if you know your child is going to have sex, educate them about contraception. Better still, provide them with what they need.

Keeping cybersex in perspective

Young children may end up coming across online porn without even looking for it. Most children are likely to use the Internet as a reference source sooner or later, so you need to arm them with balance, and even scepticism, in their approach to the online world. Discuss with them the difference between fantasy and reality. They must understand that the information they come across online is not necessarily true, and does not necessarily reflect real life.

In the virtual world as in the real world, kids need to feel confident enough not to be pressured into doing anything that makes them feel uncomfortable. We explored how to keep them safe online in Chapter 10.

Drugs, alcohol and smoking

Your child may be tempted to try drugs, alcohol and cigarettes in a bid to fit in and to feel part of the group. They may also dabble out of curiosity, or in an attempt to reduce anxiety. But while the young brain is still forming, any of these toxins can impair its development. It's advisable, therefore, to share with your child the dangers of these substances before problems arise.

Discouraging experimentation

There is no clear-cut answer on how to prevent experimentation. Many young people do not use drugs or participate in heavy drinking because they don't want to disappoint their parents. Your stance could make the difference between your child using drugs regularly, occasionally or not at all.

HOW CAN I TELL IF MY CHILD HAS BEEN TAKING DRUGS?

- ✿ They might be giggly and uncoordinated.
- ✿ Their eyes maybe bloodshot, and they may have dilated pupils.
- ✿ They might temporarily have lost their short-term memory.
- ✿ They might have drug-related items on them or in their room.
- ✿ Their clothes or bedroom might smell of marijuana.
- ✿ They might be trying to mask that smell with incense or perfume.
- ✿ They might be short of money.
- ✿ Their grades might be dropping.
- ✿ They might be rebelling at home.
- ✿ They might have mood swings, or a change in their mood.
- ✿ Their appearance might have changed.
- ✿ Their friendship groups may have changed.

Again, approaching the subject when your children are young makes a huge difference. Arm them with knowledge so they can make informed choices.

There's nothing worse than a boring lecture from the parents about the dos and don'ts of drugs. In fact, most kids know far more about the possible effects of some of the more esoteric substances than we do. But they do need to hear some home truths, and here are some attention grabbers:

- ❂ long-term excess drinking can lead to alcoholism;
- ❂ smoking turns your lungs black; and
- ❂ taking too many prescription painkillers can result in a serious overdose.

Kids take their good health for granted, so they're not going to be concerned about the distant prospect of cirrhosis of the liver when they're binge-drinking at a party. (The only warnings that might carry some sway are, for girls that smoking causes premature aging of the skin, and for boys that too much booze can hinder 'performance'.)

TOP-TEN TIPS ON HAVING 'THAT' CONVERSATION

- ❂ Plan ahead to make sure you won't be interrupted.
- ❂ Make sure you know what you're going to say.
- ❂ Be honest.
- ❂ Encourage your child to ask questions so you can have a genuine conversation.
- ❂ Highlight the risks.
- ❂ Talk about their emotions: how do they feel about this issue?

✿ Tell your child how you feel but remain calm.

✿ Listen with compassion and show unconditional love.

✿ Clarify your expectations.

✿ Agree to the ground rules.

So how can we make sure they take care of themselves? This is where a focus on consequences rather than punishment really comes into its own, but you need to know your own child and what makes them tick. If you understand your child's long- and short-term goals, you will be able to highlight how drug and alcohol misuse could interfere with their achieving these goals. Career prospects, sporting prowess, musical ambitions — substance misuse could jeopardise all these and more.

The facts that you need to set before your child, calmly and authoritatively, include the following:

✿ Many drugs are highly addictive.

✿ It is unsafe to drive while drunk OR high.

✿ Continued use of drugs or alcohol is linked to lower grades and failure at school.

✿ Drug use and heavy drinking are linked to mental illness.

✿ Smoking weed increases the likelihood of moving to harder drugs.

Persuasion is the key, but an open discussion will be a better vehicle for this than a monologue from you. The following questions might be a good starting point for initiating a dialogue:

1. What might make doing drugs an option for you?

The answers to this question might uncover issues such as peer pressure or problems with self-confidence. By keeping communication going on these topics, you might be able to address some serious anxiety in your child's life.

2. What is stopping you from doing drugs at the moment?

Their answer to this question will give you a better understanding of their present boundaries, how strong your protective influence is, and how they are coping with life in general at the moment.

As with other areas of conflict with teenagers, choose your battles — you don't want to turn their home into a war zone. When I was raising my teenagers, I carefully chose which battles to pursue. I decided that one cigarette would not kill them but that one tablet of ecstasy might. I therefore became less heavy-handed about smoking. But for me, drugs were a deal-breaker. Likewise, I knew they would be drinking, so I urged moderation rather than abstention. You will know what rules and boundaries sit best with you.

You will also know what arguments will hold most weight with your child, but I've found the following 'model answers' to be effective both with my own children and with those I've helped professionally:

> ✿ I'm not suggesting that because you're using drugs/ drinking to excess that your life is about to spin out

of control, but I want to emphasise that if someone is high or drunk, their judgement is impaired, and they might make decisions that could be harmful to them.

✿ People I know who use alcohol or drugs on a regular basis often use them to blot out how they are feeling. There are other ways of coping with your feelings. Perhaps we can talk about this.

✿ I'm happy that this is not something you're doing on a regular basis, but it can still be harmful when your brain is not yet fully developed. You say it's not a big deal, so when would it feel like a big deal? When do you feel you might need to use drugs or drink more?

✿ You say you've tried drugs/alcohol/cigarettes. I'm genuinely interested to know what it was like for you, and why you decided to give it a go.

If you suspect that your children are misusing substances regularly, you probably need to ask yourself where are they getting the money from, and how seriously involved are they — do you need outside support?

Responsibility and control

Children often feel that they don't have control over what they are doing, and that someone else is calling the shots. Helping them to discover that they have a choice will enable them to feel that they have some power, and that they can exert it. They can decide for themselves what is important for them and whether they are prepared to pass up opportunities for the sake of drink and drugs.

Helping your child understand that actions have consequences — regardless of whether they are sober, drunk, or high — can also be a powerful motivator. Don't let them play the victim if they are the worse for drink or drugs.

It can be very hard for a child to resist peer pressure to take drugs or drink. They'll find it much easier to say no if they feel in control.

Teaching your child to say no

The following formula is the best approach to saying no. Let your child know that after they've done it once, the second time will be much easier.

- Take a deep breath.
- Stand up straight.
- Drop your shoulders.
- Make eye contact.
- Say what is on your mind.
- Do not make excuses.
- Stand up for yourself.
- Where possible, walk away.

This might seem a trivial exercise whilst addressing such serious topics, but the sooner your child becomes comfortable with saying no and standing up for themselves the more resilient they will be when faced with tough decisions.

It might be useful to refer to the exercise The X-Plan, from Chapter 14, which offers a way for your child to extricate themselves from an uncomfortable situation.

∎∎∎

Your kids want to behave like adults and yet they are not adults. Experimentation is inevitable. But if your children are uninformed or misinformed, accidents and mistakes could happen — and they could be very costly ones.

These substances, by their very nature, can be hugely addictive. It is not productive as a parent, to blame yourself if your child has 'gone off the rails'. If you find yourself in the situation where your child is abusing these substances, the sooner you seek professional help and support, the better for your child and the whole family.

SEX, DRUGS AND DRINKING CHECKLIST

✿ Talk to your child about sex early — the earlier you do it the less taboo it will be.

✿ Make sure you have that conversation with them before they come across online porn.

✿ You probably can't stop them from having sex, but you can make sure they're having safe sex.

✿ Be aware of the signs of drug use.

✿ Make sure your child is aware of the potential consequences of drug and alcohol misuse.

✿ Be prepared to compromise and accept the lesser evils of occasional smoking and drinking on condition that they do not try anything riskier.

Conclusion

It's extraordinary to think that the word 'teenager' only came into use in the 1950s. Were adolescents not noticeably different to the rest of the population before that time?

Well, they certainly are now, and life with them is rarely easy — and it's not meant to be. We might find the challenges they present us with trying, but who else is going to confront us with that rare combination of raw idealism and monstrous selfishness, and remind us so vividly of how we were once?

Most families come through the storm of adolescence with all parties unscathed. But your teen will welcome anything you can do to make their journey a smoother process — even if they don't show it at the time.

The perfect 'teen-tamer' would probably have the diplomatic skills of Ban Ki-moon, the determination of the Iron Duke and the forbearance of Mother Teresa. And we all know there is no such thing as perfection. The big thing to remember is that you don't have to get this 'right, you just have to be willing to try, and to show your teen that your love for them means they are worth the effort.

So give some of these tried-and-tested techniques a go, involve your teen in the exercises you think they'd find helpful, and proceed with optimism.

Some of these exercises – and many more can be found in my free App : The Teen Toolbox. It provides more information, guidance, and inspiration and is regularly updated. To download the app - please visit your app store and search for TEEN Toolbox.

And please remember that you have a unique and valuable adult-in-waiting forming mysteriously inside that rather challenging cocoon. It's a big adventure for you both — make the most of it!

Values List

This is not an exhaustible list but serves as a guide for the exercise in Chapter X.

Acceptance	Fairness	Leadership	Security
Adventure	Faith	Love	Self-control
Ambition	Family	Loyalty	Sensitivity
Availability	Freedom		Stability
Authenticity	Focus	Mindfulness	Strength
		Modesty	Support
Balance	Generosity	Motivation	Sympathy
Belonging	Grace		
Boldness	Gratitude	Neatness	
	Guidance		Teamwork
Calmness		Obedience	Thoughtfulness
Comfort	Happiness	Open-mindedness	Trust
Consistency	Harmony	Optimism	
Cooperation	Health	Order	Understanding
Courtesy	Helpfulness	Organisation	Unity
	Honesty		
Dependability		Peace	Variety
Dignity	Imagination	Perfection	Vision
Direction	Impartiality	Perseverance	
Discipline	Independence	Power	Warmth
Duty	Integrity	Privacy	Wisdom
	Intuition		Wittiness
Empathy		Reasonableness	
Encouragement	Joy	Recreation	
Energy	Justice	Reliability	Youthfulness
Enjoyment		Resilience	
Excellence	Kindness	Respect	

The Author

Cai Graham is a parent, coach, and founder of Peak Parenting. She has a degree in Business and was an IT project manager until she became a mother and spent some years focused on nurturing her family.

Once her children were in senior school, Cai set up her first passion-based business as a family photographer. From observing families, she noticed a modern-day epidemic of parents *enduring* their kids instead of enjoying their kids, and feeling overwhelmed navigating the trials of modern parenthood.

Cai felt inspired to support parents and children to reach a new level of love, understanding and unity within the home; she blended my 20+ years of motherhood with her background as a therapist, coach and photographer to create an online education program, a book, and luxury retreats. She specialises in supporting families through crisis, healing families who have experienced trauma and loss, and overcoming obstacles so they can enjoy a bright future.

Cai's mission is to empower parents and teenagers with the tools to navigate adolescence through confidence and effective communication, so they can live full, happy and healthy lives.

Website: www.caigraham.com
Facebook: www.facebook.com/caigraham
Twitter: @caigraham
LinkedIn: www.linkedin.com/caigraham
YouTube: Cai Graham
Free App :   TEEN Toolbox

Printed in Great Britain
by Amazon

57194181R00115